THE OTHER KUWAIT

D1508902

An American Father and Daughter's
Personal Impressions

Lee R. Lambert
Erin Lambert

Publisher:
Lee R. Lambert & Associates Publishing
Worthington, Ohio

THE OTHER KUWAIT
An American Father and Daughter's Personal Impressions

Cover Graphic Design by: Adnan Al-Abdulmuhsen

Title by: Marnie C. Lambert

ISBN Number: 0-9626397-1-0

LCCC Number: 91-093116

Printed in the United States of America

CONTENTS

DEDICATION

This book is dedicated to our best friend, Carolyn Lambert. As the wife and mother in the Lambert family, she has been the glue that has held us together for over a quarter of a century. Without her persuasiveness, persistence, perseverance and patience, this book would never have been written.

PREFACE

We have known about "The Other Kuwait" for ten years. But, the Kuwait we have come to know during our many visits never seems to be the same Kuwait we read about in the newspaper and magazine articles or see and hear about on American television programs. We have wanted to share our personal impressions of Kuwait for a long time. Our dormant seed of inspiration has at last germinated. The harvest has been completed. Without ever knowing it, Iraq and its ruthless President, Saddam Hussein, provided the motivation. Frequent distortion and half-truths by the world media solidified our dedication and our family joined us in contributing the needed perspiration. But, most importantly, let us never forget that Kuwait - - and only Kuwait - - can take the credit for the heartwarming story.

INTRODUCTION

Lee R. Lambert

The seeds for this book were sown on a Monday morning nearly a decade ago during a Kuwait sponsored educational seminar being conducted at a retreat location nestled in a heavily wooded and quietly secluded site only a stone's throw from the University of Washington's Seattle campus.

It was September of 1983. A steady drizzle of rain fell from the gray sky. Each rain drop was filtered by thousands of deciduous leaves and pine needles before reaching the lush carpet of green surrounding our single-story, cottage-style training facility. Although typical of the Pacific Northwest, the setting presented a stark contrast from the treeless, sun-parched desert surroundings my Kuwaiti students had left fewer than 24 hours before.

I was the seminar leader charged with the responsibility of transferring knowledge to the participants. When I took the platform to begin my first encounter with this group of twenty well-groomed Kuwaiti business executives, I was admittedly apprehensive. This was to be my first "all foreign" student body and I wasn't certain what to expect. Would they understand me? Would I understand them? Would the stories and examples I had used so effectively with American audiences be relevant to Kuwaiti applications? These questions were clearly on my mind as I took my position on the training platform.

I peered out over the lectern. As my eyes darted from face to face, I could not help noticing that each man sported a mustache. There were as many different styles and types of mustaches as there were men. Some were thick and bushy like Tom Selleck's, and some were thin and neatly groomed like Wayne Newton's. Instantly my mind flashed back to my days as a newspaper sportswriter covering the Oakland Athletics Major League Baseball team in the mid-1970s. At that time, all 25 players on owner Charley Finley's eccentric, but frighteningly successful, team proudly sported full, bushy mustaches. In those days it was understood: if you were an Oakland "A," you had a mustache. I naively assumed, then, that the mustache look must be a "Kuwaiti thing," but for some reason, it was years later before I bothered to inquire about the significance. When I finally did ask, I learned that whether a man wore a mustache or not was essentially a personal choice and that many of the Kuwaiti men felt the mustache enhanced their appearances.

I later realized that in its own small way, the mustache example illustrates how quickly we notice differences in appearances, traditions, and culture, but how reluctant we are to take the time to learn the significance and history behind these differences. Instead we tend to form opinions and draw conclusions based on very limited factual information, and, in so doing we limit our understanding of the larger world in which we live.

From that first day of instruction, it was abundantly clear to me that my week in Seattle was going to be a memorable experience. We began the seminar with the customary introductions. Thankfully, one of my major concerns was quickly dispelled as I learned that all of the men spoke English extremely well, although the heavy Arab accents severely taxed my listening skills. I noticed the men were all about the same age, they were dressed in similar clothing, and they all had thick dark hair and dark eyes. In fact, I remember thinking, "They all look exactly alike," and it seemed at the time that everyone was named either Mohammed or Ali.

The training subject for the week was project management, not exactly a stimulating topic, guaranteed to keep students on the edges of their seats. Acutely aware of the "dryness" of the material, I, as always, injected a heavy dose of humor into the presentation. Within the first few hours of the program, I was pleasantly surprised to learn that Kuwaiti men possess an active sense of humor. Not only did the students laugh at my jokes (sometimes out of courtesy I'm sure), but they also willingly shared anecdotes from their personal experiences in Kuwait. By noon on that first day, I knew I had made twenty new friends.

These new friends also happened to be intelligent and challenging students. As a group, they were inquisitive, ambitious, and eager to absorb the information. It was obvious from their almost uncontrolled enthusiasm that their youthful optimism was yet to be tempered by the experiences and stark realities of the business world. However, their excitement and positive attitudes were infectious; and this attitude, mixed with excellent probing questions and their directly applicable analogies, contributed heavily to one of the most enjoyable and productive teaching experiences of my career.

For me, Friday came too soon. By the end of our week together I wasn't sure who had learned more - - my students or I. I sincerely regretted that my time with these visitors from Kuwait had come to an end. That afternoon in Seattle, as we reluctantly exchanged good-byes, was one of the rare occasions in my life when I have actually been speechless.

Fortunately, since that initial exposure in Seattle, fate has allowed my family and me dozens of opportunities, both personal and professional, to get to know Kuwaiti people throughout the United States, Great Britain and Canada as well as "on location" in Kuwait. As an off-spring of these frequent opportunities, my heart has relentlessly encouraged my mind to explore and share the uniqueness of Kuwait in a book that others, who may never have the chance to know Kuwait and its wonderful people "up close and personal" as we have, can enjoy and use to create their own mental images of this unique Middle Eastern country.

Over the years my enthusiasm for this book project has been, like the ocean's tide, constantly in a state of flux - - high one moment and low the next. Frequent verbal commitments uttered to friends and family pledging to write "my Kuwait book" became empty promises, as nothing ever seemed to appear on paper. Family members tired of the constant rhetoric. Eventually, whenever I mentioned my cherished project, I was either completely ignored or sarcastically chided, "We'll believe it when we see it!"

I honestly tried. I had written parts of this book several times over in my head, but each time I became serious about actually starting, each time I sat down at the computer to compose my verbal masterpiece of information graphically describing Kuwait and its people, something would happen. My burning motivation and fiery enthusiasm would be inevitably extinguished by a flood of other tasks - - tasks that, for one reason or another, commanded a higher priority. Finally, ruthless self diagnosis to isolate the cause of my repeated inability to devote attention to producing this badly needed book was successful. The symptoms were shockingly obvious. I was suffering from a severe case of procrastination, otherwise known as the dreaded "I'll-Do-It-Tomorrow Syndrome." Thinking back, I was reluctantly forced to admit that many of my other projects, especially the simple "fix-it" jobs my wife, Carolyn, frequently begged me to complete around the house, had died from precisely the same affliction.

In the morning hours of August 2, 1990, however, my procrastination was miraculously cured. Iraq's unprecedented invasion and brutal occupation of a stunned and helpless Kuwait provided the antidote for my debilitating personality trait. With each graphically reported Iraqi atrocity against the peaceful people of the desert oasis I had come to love, my resolve was strengthened to finally tell my "Kuwait story."

In the weeks following the invasion, as the American Congress' debate over the Iraqi occupation of Kuwait became increasingly heated, with some members challenging Kuwait's worthiness to receive the benefit of American intervention, the long-standing need for this book became dramatically clear to me. And, as if to further solidify my commitment, each time I opened the newspaper what seemed like a never-ending stream of half-truths and inaccuracies - - even outright lies - - about Kuwait flowed like a raging river of bogus black print, threatening to wash away all record of what I knew as the real Kuwait. Discussions with friends and neighbors further verified in my mind the need for the real story to be told, as their comments and questions - - based on available information - - highlighted the absurdity of popular misconceptions about Kuwait.

Through the book, I convinced myself I could construct a dam that would put a stop to this relentless flood of confusing misinformation which pervaded the press coverage. My mind, which many claim is normally cluttered with insignificant odds and ends, became crystal clear and sharply focused on my objectives: to correct misconceptions and eliminate misrepresentations through the presentation of factual, accurate, and timely information and to tell the real story of Kuwait in a personal way, as seen through the eyes of an American family.

This book, then, based on an average American family's real life experiences while visiting in Kuwait and working with Kuwaitis, will attempt to paint a vivid picture of life in Kuwait. And when the reader has completed his intellectual journey through this now-famous Arab Emirate, I hope it will be obvious, as it is to us, why this relatively tiny patch of desert, its fascinating people, and their ancient traditions were, and always will be, worth saving.

INTRODUCTION

Erin Lambert

In the afternoon of August 2nd, 1990, after spending hours with our eyes practically glued to television's Cable News Network's reporting on Iraq's invasion of Kuwait, my family and I ventured outside into the glorious Ohio summer sun. We knew that we must try to clear our minds of this devastating news and that a day sunning ourselves at the pool would be just the cure. Although we knew the Worthington Hills Country Club, less than a mile away, would be stirring with anxiety over the previous night's shocking military action against Kuwait, we gathered our beach towels and headed out the door.

Because we had many Kuwaiti friends and business associates, this was an especially sad day for our family, and we expected questions of all kinds from our concerned friends. We braced ourselves for many of these questions, but we could never have anticipated the one asked by my good friend Elizabeth Coleman. I had known Elizabeth since third grade, and had responded to a lot of her "interesting" questions. But, none have surprised me more than the one she asked me on August 2nd.

As I entered through the club gate, I saw Elizabeth playing tennis with a friend. She noticed me immediately and began walking quickly in my direction with an eager expression on her face. I was sure she wanted to hear the details about last night's terrible news from Kuwait. While still a tennis court away, her curiosity got the best of her. Elizabeth simply could not wait, so she stopped and yelled, "Hey, Erin, did you hear that Julia Roberts got her hair cut?" I was shocked. I could not believe my ears; surely she was joking. Was it possible that in Elizabeth's mind Julia Roberts' new hair style could have taken precedent over Iraq's invasion of Kuwait? I found this very hard to comprehend. I answered Elizabeth somewhat indignantly, "No, I didn't know that Julia Roberts got her hair cut." I quickly added, "I guess I was a little preoccupied with Iraq's invasion of Kuwait."[1]

Now it was Elizabeth's turn to be shocked. Her reaction to this news made it clear that she honestly had no idea that Kuwait had been invaded. At that time, I remember being amazed by my blond friend's obliviousness to important world events, but now, as I look back on the situation, Elizabeth was not the only person who did not have a "clue" about Kuwait. In fact, since my first trip in 1986, I remember each time I returned from a journey to the Middle East, having to endure a heavy cross-fire of questions concerning Kuwait: "Do they really eat camels?" or, "Since you are a girl, you aren't allowed to go outside there, are you?" or, "You have to always cover your whole body and head there, don't you?"

The questions always came fast and furiously, each one a little more bizarre than the one preceding it. I have always attempted to answer the questions, no matter how unusual they were. I feel it is very important for Americans to understand Kuwait, and I hope, with the help of this book and the worldwide attention generated by Iraq's invasion, that unfamiliarity with a wonderful country like Kuwait will never again plague the people of my own country.

---

[1] An article in the Life Section of the January 22, 1992 issue of U.S.A. Today indicated that during 1991 Julia Roberts, one of America's most famous young actresses, received more front page newspaper and magazine coverage than any other news topic - - including the Gulf War and the break-up of the former Union of Soviet Socialist Republics (USSR).

Through the years I have personally observed and become friends with many Kuwaiti citizens, and I find them fun-loving, patriotic, family-oriented people with morals, values and traditions remarkably parallel to those of Americans. On each of my trips to Kuwait I am consistently overwhelmed by the insights to be gained and the knowledge to be absorbed during a single evening meal with a Kuwaiti family. The people of Kuwait relish the opportunity to entertain visitors who show a sincere interest in their history, culture and religion. Now, through this book, readers have an opportunity to join me and my family for an "evening meal" learning experience in Kuwait where they will hear Kuwait's remarkable story along with the Lambert family's favorite recollections about the Kuwaiti people and their unique culture.

KUWAIT "AT-A-GLANCE"

History:
> Settled by Utab tribe in approximately 1710. State of Kuwait Constitution ratified in 1962.

Location:
> Middle East surrounded by Iraq, Iran, Saudi Arabia and the Arabian Gulf.

Size:
> Land mass of 6,877 square miles (two-thirds the size of the State of Maryland).

Topography:
> Flat, baron sandy desert.

Climate:
> Long hot, dry summers. Short, warm and sometimes rainy winters.

Form of Government:
> Hereditary Emirate. Operates under The Constitution of the State of Kuwait written in 1962. (Based on democratic principles).

Population:
> 1.5 million (2.1 million before Iraq invasion) - - approximately 830,000 Kuwaiti citizens.

Religion:
> Islam

Language:
> Arabic (unofficial second language is English).

Economic Base:
> Oil, oil by-products and investments. ($30 billion Gross National Product in 1989).

Education System:
> Public and Private. Compulsory to age 18. Free education through university level.

Architecture:
> Mix of traditional Arab and modern high rise office buildings and large private family residences.

KUWAIT: A REVERSE CHRONOLOGY OF KUWAIT'S SIGNIFICANT EVENTS

February 27, 1992: Celebration of one year anniversary of Kuwait's liberation from Iraqi occupation.

November 6, 1991: Last of 751 burning or damaged oil wells was capped.

March 14, 1991: Kuwait's Amir, Sheikh Jaber Al-Ahmad Al-Jaber Al-Sabah, returned to his homeland after seven-and-a-half months in exile.

March 11, 1991: Iraq renounced its annexation of Kuwait in a letter to U.N. Secretary-General Perez de Cuellar.

February 27, 1991: Kuwait was liberated from Iraqi occupation by Allied Coalition military forces under the auspices of the United Nations.

February 23, 1991: Coalition military forces initiated a ground campaign against Iraq.

January 16, 1991: Coalition military forces declared war against Iraq and initiated a massive air campaign.

November, 1990: The United Nations authorized use of "all necessary means" to remove Iraq from Kuwait after January 15, 1991.

October, 1990: The Kuwaiti People's Conference was conducted in Saudi Arabia.

August 2, 1990: Iraq invaded and occupied Kuwait.

July, 1990: Elections were held to establish a new consultative National Assembly.

July, 1987: The United States "reflagged" Kuwaiti oil tankers as a protective measure against random Iran-Iraq war-related violence.

January, 1987: The Fifth Islamic Conference was hosted by Kuwait.

July, 1986: The National Assembly of Kuwait was dissolved.

February, 1986: The Silver Anniversary (25th) of Kuwaiti independence was celebrated.

May, 1985: An unsuccessful car bomb assassination was attempted on His Highness the Amir, Sheikh Jaber Al-Ahmad Al-Jaber Al-Sabah.

February, 1983: The *Dar Al-Athar Al-Islamiyyah* (The Museum of Islamic Arts) opened as part of the Kuwait National Museum.

August, 1982: Crash of the *Souk Al-Manakh* (secondary stock exchange market) sent the Kuwait economy into severe downturn.

February, 1981: Elections were held to establish a new National Assembly of Kuwait.

May, 1981: Kuwait joined the Gulf Cooperation Council (GCC).

December, 1976: The Kuwait Foundation for the Advancement of Sciences (KFAS) was established.

1976: The Fund for Future Generations was established and ten percent of all State revenue each year is set aside for the benefit of future generations).

August, 1976: The National Assembly of Kuwait was dissolved.

March, 1975: The Kuwaiti government acquired total ownership of Kuwait Oil Company.

1971: The Kuwait Institute for Scientific Research (KISR) was opened.

April, 1969: The Central Bank of Kuwait was formed.

November, 1966: The Kuwait University was officially dedicated.

1966: Kuwait and Saudi Arabia agreed on the boundaries for the Neutral Zone.

May, 1963: Kuwait joined the United Nations.

January, 1963: Kuwait's first elected National Assembly was convened.

November 11, 1962: The Constitution of Kuwait was ratified by His Highness the Amir, Sheikh Jaber Al-Ahmad Al-Jaber Al-Sabah.

July, 1961: Kuwait becomes a member of the Arab League.

June 19, 1961: Kuwait declared its independence from Great Britian.

April, 1961: The Kuwaiti Dinar became Kuwait's official currency.

1960: The Organization of Petroleum Exporting Countries (OPEC) was established with Kuwait among the founding 13 nations.

1960: The first Kuwaiti woman was employed by Kuwait Oil Company.

1957: All of Kuwait's ancient protective walls were demolished. Only five massive entry gates were preserved.

1952: The first Kuwait Masterplan was developed.

May, 1951: Kuwait Radio began operation.

June, 1946: The first shipment of Kuwait crude oil was exported.

February, 1938: The massive Burgan oil field was discovered.

1932: The modern boundaries between Saudi Arabia, Iraq, and the State of Kuwait were set to be consistent with those originally delineated in a May, 1922 British-sponsored conference.

1920: The third and final wall around Kuwait City was built.

December, 1911: Kuwait opened its first formal school, the AL-Mubarakiya School.

January, 1899: A Friendship and Cooperation Treaty (known as the Exclusive Agreement) was signed with Great Britian.

1886: The first Kuwait currency was minted in copper and distributed.

1773: Kuwait was the victim of an epidemic that killed more than half of its inhabitants.

1765: A Danish traveler, Karsten Niebuhr, placed Kuwait (referred to as "Grane") on the map.

1756: Sheikh Sabah Bin Jaber was elected as the First Ruler (Amir) of Kuwait.

1710 (approximately): The Utab tribe and the Al-Sabah family arrived in Kuwait.

RULERS OF KUWAIT:

1978 -	Sheikh Jaber Al-Ahmad Al-Sabah
1965 - 1977	Sheikh Sabah AL-Salem Al-Sabah
1950 - 1965	Sheikh Abdullah Al-Salem Al-Sabah
1921 - 1950	Sheikh Ahmad Al-Jaber Al-Sabah
1917 - 1921	Sheikh Salim Al-Mubarak
1915 - 1917	Sheikh Jaber II
1896 - 1915	Sheikh Mubarak Al-Sabah
1892 - 1896	Sheikh Muhammad I
1866 - 1892	Sheikh Abdullah II
1859 - 1866	Sheikh Sabah II
1812 - 1859	Sheikh Jaber I
1762 - 1812	Sheikh Abdullah I
1756 - 1762	Sheikh Sabah Bin Jaber

KUWAIT CABINET POSITIONS

Crown Prince/Prime Minister
Deputy Prime Minister/Minister of Foreign Affairs
Minister of Defense
Minister of Interior
Minister of Information
Minister of Finance
Minister of Oil
Minister of Planning
Minister of Islamic Affairs
Minister of Justice
Minister of Education
Minister of Public Works
Minister of State for Municipality Affairs
Minister of Higher Education
Minister of State for Housing Affairs
Minister of Commerce and Industry
Minister of Electricity and Water
Minister of Public Health
Minister of Communication
Minister of State for Cabinet Affairs

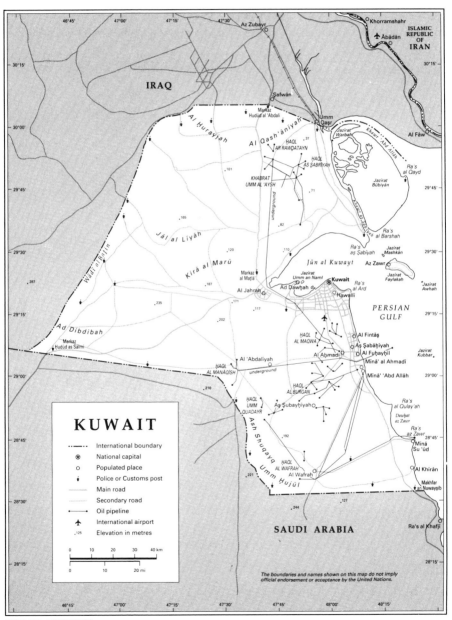

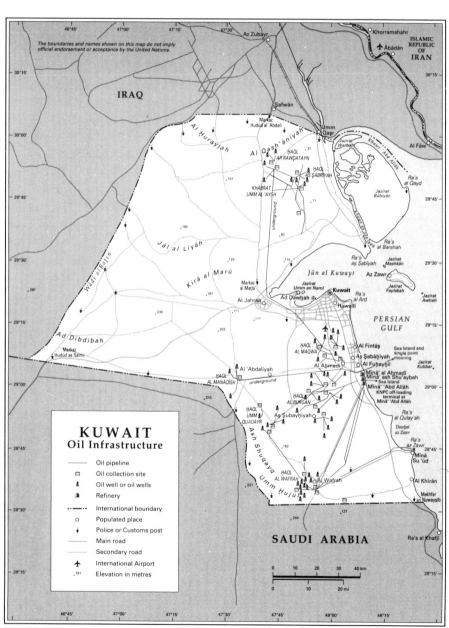

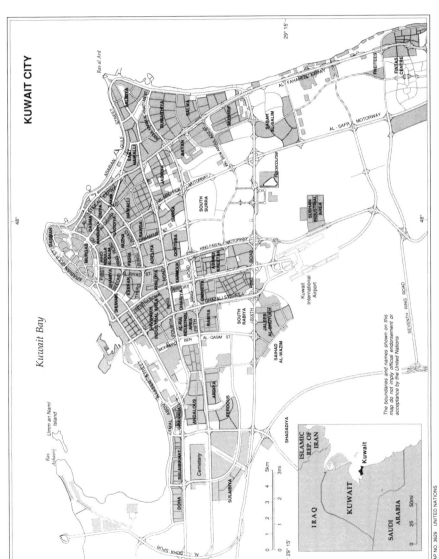

1

THE AMERICAN IMAGE OF KUWAIT

They Live in Tents, But Drive Mercedes

Erin Lambert

"The world is governed more by appearances than by realities, so that it is fully as necessary to seem to know something as to know it."

Daniel Webster

My family's personal experiences inside the country of Kuwait and our close observations of the Kuwaiti people during the past five years have made us acutely sensitive to just how badly Arabs in general, and Kuwaitis in particular, are misunderstood in the United States.

Unfortunately, the limited educational material concerning Kuwait that is available to the American public, combined with the often grossly distorted or incomplete media coverage, has resulted in the American people embracing some unimaginable, and often painfully inaccurate, perceptions and images of Kuwait and its people.

For example, in 1986 a classmate of mine in Worthington, Ohio, heard that I would be traveling to Kuwait. One day after school, while I was searching through my locker for a book, she matter-of-factly informed me that while I was in Kuwait, I should be prepared to sleep in a tent. She went on to explain that her father had recently been to Kuwait on business; and, when he returned, he informed her, "The Kuwaitis live in tents, but drive Mercedes."

I was surprised at this news. My dad had not warned me that conditions in Kuwait would be so primitive. I thanked my friend for her worthwhile advice.

Upon my return from Kuwait, I was eager to seek out my friend and correct her. Her father, as it turned out, had been so busy conducting his business in this oil rich country, he had not taken the time to learn anything about the people or their way of life.

Yes, there are tents set up in the desert sand, and, yes, there are Mercedes parked in front of the tents. But no, the Kuwaiti people do not live in these tents. The Kuwaitis do, however, use tents in the desert sand in exactly the same manner as we Americans use tents in the mountains - - as part of a relaxing camping trip away from the hustle and bustle of the big city.

At the time, I hoped that this "tent and Mercedes" story was an isolated case of misinformation; but, as time passed, I began to realize that the Kuwaiti "perception problem" was much worse than I first realized.

In an attempt to verify for myself (and eventually to demonstrate for readers) exactly how ludicrous and misleading these common misperceptions have become, I embarked upon the task of conducting an informal survey entitled, "What Do You Think You Know About Kuwait?"

First, I developed several surveys with different questions for a variety of age groups in the form of loosely structured, open-ended questions which I hoped would elicit more than simple "yes or no" answers. A large cross-section of Ohio school-age children, ranging in ages from ten to eighteen years, was polled approximately one month after the Coalition forces began the air raids on Baghdad in mid-January, 1990, and after teachers had spent months informing students about Kuwait. (I can't imagine what the answers would have been prior to the invasion.) These age groups were intentionally selected. In my opinion, youth hold the key to the world's future; therefore, the perceptions they have now will help shape the world of tomorrow. Reality, as this age group perceives or imagines it, will have a strong influence on their soon-to-be adult attitudes and opinions.

Many of the mental images of life in Kuwait revealed in the survey are so distinctly different from reality, so ridiculously absurd, that they are genuinely comical. In fact,if so many did not actually believe the outlandish stories, the answers I gathered would have been absolutely hilarious.

Below, I have selected some of the more far-fetched survey responses as illustrations of how vast the differences between reality and perception can be. Readers should note that each answer is provided exactly as written by children (including spelling); absolutely no changes have been made to the responses they provided.

When asked, "Where in the world is Kuwait?" a ten year old girl replied simply, "Eurpe?" Two eleven year old boys, however, gave a bit more detail answering, "Kuwait is near in the middle east in Ashia. Some countries by it are Saudi Arabis, Iraq, Iran and Greece"; and "Kuwait is in Irock. Near Isral, Soti Arabia." The same boy's female classmate was certain Kuwait was "Middle Germeny and Irac."

"What language is spoken in Kuwait?" seemed like an easy question, but the answers surprised me. Seventy percent of the elementary students surveyed were positive that the Kuwaiti people spoke Spanish.

Other languages credited to the Kuwaitis by this younger generation were African, Portuguese, German, Indian, Russian, Hebrew, Turkish, Iranian, and Iraqi. Most of the older children answered correctly (Arabic), and one twelve year old girl was close when she penciled in "Irabit."

A confident eleven year old girl answered my inquiry, "How does the Kuwaiti government earn money?", stating, "They earn their money by taxes and maybe by stealing." She concluded, "I picture them mean or selling drugs, maybe." The majority of the responses to this question reflected the children's knowledge of the American system of raising money through taxation. Very few suggested Kuwait's government made the majority of its money through the sale of oil and oil products.

Since the Islamic religion is such a big part of a Kuwaiti's life, I was anxious to learn the American youth's level of knowledge on this topic, so I asked, "What do you know about the Islamic religion?"

The most interesting responses to this question came from the boys and girls in the 14-18 year old age range. The oldest respondent, a boy of eighteen, indicated, "They believe in God. Not our God, a weird one, Allah." One seventeen year old girl thought. "They believe in a few Gods." Another seventeen year old girl explained her thinking saying, "They don't tolerate other religions and that's partly why they are so immature about people not like them." The answer I got which perhaps best reflected the seriousness of the American's misconceptions about the Islamic religion came from a fourteen year old girl, who shared her knowledge that, "The Muslims believe that the cow is sacred and they worship Muhammed."

I was sure my Kuwaiti friends would be happy to

learn what the young Americans think they eat. Among the preferred food items of Kuwaitis, in the minds of those who responded to my survey, were snakes, lizards, camels, dogs and cats. One young man thought Kuwaitis eat a lot of Mexican food and another suggested they drink gallons of wine. A few accurately named rice, fish, fruit, and bread among the Kuwaitis' favorites.

Some say kids are the same throughout the world, so I thought it would be interesting to ask, "What do kids do for fun on the weekends in Kuwait?" The answers were definitely interesting. One of the older survey participants, an eighteen year old boy, was sure he knew the answer, "They get wasted (drunk) and cause trouble just like us." Other answers to this question demonstrated the impact of the war that was being waged in the Arabian Gulf at the time the survey was conducted. One youngster said, "I think they play inside because if they played outside they might get bombed." Another thought, "They do nothing. They have to work and be safe from bombs also." One twelve year old girl said simply, "They learn to fight."

My question, "How are Kuwaiti schools different from American schools?", generated some informative replies. "Low budget and very mean teachers," said one boy in the sixth grade, while his female classmate added, "We can say the Pledge of Allegiance and we have our freedom. They don't." A high school girl indicated, "I think they get punished with objects when they do something bad." Finally, a boy in elementary school, obviously influenced by current events, thought, "They probably practice going to shelters in case Iraq attacks."

The last two questions of the survey, "What do you know about the government and law in Kuwait?" and "What do you know about marriage and family life in Kuwait?", produced some of the more absurd and clearly misinformed responses.

I have focused on the feedback provided by the high school age group because I was most disappointed by their lack of accurate knowledge and understanding. In the area of government and law, some of the answers were as follows: "A lot of leaders have been killed or have resigned because they were afraid of getting killed."; "If you steal, they cut off your fingers."; "I don't know anything about it, except it is communist"; "The leader is a Shick, who has many wives and children"; and, "It is a dictatorship run by a select few, with a few rich living there, and many poor who are treated as slaves."

As for the subjects of marriage and family life, the answers were no less disconcerting. The American students provided a variety of unusual replies including: "A man can have twelve wives. You have to buy or trade for your wife or wives - - like 10 pigs and a $1,000"; "Parents are mean and their father is probably in the army"; "It [marriage] doesn't have to be legal"; "They can have five wives, livestock pays for the wife"; "They can have as many wives as they want. They just give each other rings and they're married"; "Every man may have five wives. The children's mom may not talk to them"; "The women aren't allowed to look their kids in the eye"; "A woman can't be seen in public with a man"; "Neither parents can talk to the first born child"; "Brothers and sisters marry each other"; and finally, "The men can have as many wives as they please and when the men get their wives they can do whatever they want with them."

Most of the survey responses added to my uneasy feeling about how much Americans know and understand about Kuwait; however, the answer which most accurately summarized and represented my concerns regarding common American misconceptions and lack of knowledge about Kuwait came from a sixteen year old girl, who, in all honesty said simply, "I don't know anything about the culture or customs of Kuwait. I never even heard of it before the war."

It is my sincere hope that when the reader has finished reading this book, a great deal of progress will have been made toward my goal of eliminating this serious American lack of knowledge and correcting, or at least clarifying, the seemingly countless misperceptions about Kuwait.

2

AN HISTORICAL OVERVIEW OF KUWAIT

Aladdin's Lamp of the Middle East

Lee R. Lambert

"Fellow citizens, we cannot escape history."

Abraham Lincoln

The State of Kuwait, referred to in the May, 1969 issue of *National Geographic* as "Kuwait, Aladdin's Lamp of the Middle East," implying that whatever a Kuwaiti wished for could be his, is situated in the northwestern tip of the Arabian[2] Gulf. (See map page xxv.) It lies north of the Equator at approximately the same latitude (28° north) as Tampa, Florida and Corpus Christi, Texas. This strategic Middle Eastern location has resulted in Kuwait becoming a natural transportation and navigation inlet and outlet, meeting many of the import and export needs of the northeastern portion of the Arabian Peninsula.

The social and economic influence and importance of Kuwait in the region is much greater than its actual physical size would ever suggest. Including the Neutral Zone, which is shared equally with Saudi Arabia, the total area of Kuwait is about 6,877 square miles, or about two-thirds the size of the State of Maryland. A comparison with Alaska's 570,833 square miles

---

[2] Most countries of the world use the Persian Gulf designation, however, the Arabs prefer to call this body of water the Arabian Gulf and have so denoted it on maps produced within the Arab world.

of land mass shows that you could put 83 countries the size of Kuwait within America's largest state and still have room for a few football stadiums. Sorry, Texans, your proud Lone Star State could accommodate only about 39 Kuwaits.

Topographically, Kuwait is primarily barren, flat desert with some hilly terrain in the western portion of the emirate. In this arid region of Arabia, the climate is extremely dry, receiving an average of only six to seven inches of rainfall each year. The annual quantity of rain in Kuwait is comparable to the United States' driest state, Nevada, where the average annual precipitation is about 7.5 inches.

As would be expected, the temperatures in this desolate region can reach incredible highs in summer. While the average summer temperature is 105° F., it is not unusual to see the mercury climb to more than 120° F. in July and August. In late August and throughout most of September, Kuwait's weather becomes almost tropical as high humidity sets in, making it seem even hotter than it is. In the dead of winter (January) the mean temperature is a much more comfortable 40° F.

Now, in order to begin to get a better understanding of Kuwait, let your mind take a journey back in time. Your mental destination: July 4, 1776, perhaps the most important single day in American history. On that day thirteen American colonies declared their independence from British rule, and the United States, considered by many as the greatest country in the world, was officially born. It would be nearly 200 years later, on June 19, 1961, under much less dramatic circumstances, that Kuwait would establish a significant common bond with the United States when it also declared complete independence from Great Britain and discontinued its sixty year old status as a British Protectorate.[3] The result of that 1961 declaration was the birth of the modern state of Kuwait. Ten years later the United Arab Emirates[4] followed the example of its neighbor and became the last Middle East entity to end its reliance on Great Britian.

During the 1700s, however, while the American colonists were engaged in a war for independence, Kuwait City was struggling to become a successful, self-sustaining community. Karsten Niebuhr, a Danish explorer charting the territory for the Dutch and English East India Trading Companies, is said to have first identified Kuwait on a chart or map in 1765. Most historians agree, however, that Niebuhr's recognition of Kuwait as a political entity more likely marked the rise of the city to prominence, not the date that Kuwait City was first established. When Niebuhr put the city on the map, it was already rapidly adding to its population of over 10,000 people.

Early records maintained by the English East India Company set the date for the founding of Kuwait City at 1716. However, that date is challenged by traditional Kuwaiti historians, who believe that the city was in existence somewhat earlier. No reliable evidence has been found to support their claim, but according to stories I have been told, which were handed down through many generations of Kuwaitis, the year 1710 is frequently suggested as the actual date for the founding

---

[3] The British have long had a presence in the Gulf. As early as 1798 a treaty of friendship was forged with Oman and in 1853 Great Britain signed a maritime truce with the sheikdoms that presently comprise the United Arab Emirates (UAE).

[4] Covering a land mass approximately the size of Maine with a population of one million, the United Arab Emirates is composed of seven small and relatively autonomous sheikdoms; Abu Dhabi, Dubai, Sharjah, Ras Al-Khaimah, Ajman, Umm Al-Qaiwain and Fugairah. The UAE gained independence from Great Britain in 1971.

of Kuwait City.

Obviously, the cultural history of the area now occupied by Kuwait dates back considerably further. The most significant early references to Kuwait can be found in Greek history's account of a voyage of Alexander the Great's Admiral Nearchos. Nearchos sailed up the Gulf on his way to India. En route he stopped at an island called Ikaros. This island has been identified as Kuwait's modern day Failaka Island, where recent excavations have uncovered proof of a Greek trading colony, active from the third to the first century B.C. These excavations of Failaka Island unearthed an ancient Temple of Artemis, military fortifications and well-planned dwellings and workshops. Other findings on Failaka Island include stone seals from the late Bronze Age (c.3000-2100 B.C.), which indicate human presence long before the Greeks arrived.

Regardless of the exact date historians set for the founding of Kuwait City, the facts surrounding its establishment remain undisputed. At the time, (early 18th century) severe famine and drought plagued the interior of the Arabian Peninsula. Eventually, nomadic Arab tribesmen and their families were forced to leave their tents and make-shift homes, with their camels and goats in tow, in search of a new beginning. Among these nomadic Bedouin[5] tribes were the Utabs, a division of the Anaza tribe from an area known as Haddar in the Al-Aflaj region of the Najd, the area now known as Saudi Arabia.

After enduring incredible hardships in their journey from the desert's severe heat, lack of drinking water, and vicious sand storms, the Utabs came upon a

---

[5] Bedouin literally means "desert dweller" and is derived from the French version of the Arab word "badwai."

large, spectacular deep water bay on the Arabian Gulf. Although there was only a small amount of fresh spring water suitable for drinking and the sandy soil was clearly no better than that which the Utabs had reluctantly left behind, this beautiful spot on what is now known as Kuwait Bay was declared their new home. Perhaps these Bedouins had grown weary of searching for a better homeland and were satisfied to settle on the shores of this vast, natural salt water harbor. Like the American pioneers of the early 1800s, the Utab tribe "staked their claim" to the land and immediately set about establishing what would eventually become one of the most modern cities of the Middle East.

Among those early settlers were members of the Al-Sabah family, which has officially ruled Kuwait since 1756, twenty years prior to the American Revolution. Early historical accounts by European travelers refer to the ruler of Kuwait as the "Sheikh (pronounced 'shake') of Kuwait" or the "Governor of Kuwait," but today Kuwait's Head of State is known officially as "His Highness the Amir."[6]

Being chosen by the people of Kuwait in 1756 to guide the affairs of this rapidly growing city and to insure that justice was administered fairly to all was the highest honor that could have been bestowed upon the first recognized leader of Kuwait, Sheikh Sabah Bin Jaber. His selection by popular vote in the typical manner of tribal council election clearly demonstrated that he had earned his fellow tribesmen's highest level of respect and trust. Sheikh Sabah Bin Jaber faithfully served his people until 1762. In the succeeding two

---

[6] Amir is the Arabic word for "prince" and is the official title given to Kuwait's royal rulers. The most common Western spelling is "Emir," but the preferred spelling in Kuwait is Amir.

centuries, twelve other members of the Al-Sabah family have devoted themselves to the ultimate service of their people by ascending to the position of Amir.

The current Amir (1992), Sheikh Jaber Al-Ahmed Al-Jaber Al-Sabah,[7] together with his supporting government, has charted a comprehensive course of action since 1978 which has led Kuwait to some of its greatest achievements. Since the conclusion of the devastating 1990-91 war in the Gulf, the Amir has recommitted himself and his Cabinet to providing the leadership necessary to accomplish Kuwait's reconstruction and lead the country to even greater heights of achievement and democracy.

In the beginning, though, it was the vision of Sheikh Sabah Bin Jaber which resulted in the people of Kuwait taking full advantage of their strategic location on the Arabian Gulf. His countrymen quickly became known for their prowess as fishermen, pearl divers, boat builders, and shrewd merchants. Thanks to the constant encouragement of the Sheikh, Kuwait became a vital port city with its residents reaping substantial profits from the passengers and merchandise being transported to a variety of inland destinations in Persia, India, and the Ottoman Empire.

The transformation from impoverished nomadic tribesmen to respected and prosperous merchants and businessmen did not happen overnight. The Al-Sabah family has provided a seldom-equaled governmental continuity with only the Saud family in Saudi Arabia having been in power longer. This consistency and dedication have been critical in sustaining the growth of Kuwait and in achieving its evolution to a proud

---

[7] Kuwait's current Amir is the third son of Ahmad Al-Jaber Al-Sabah, the 10th Al-Sabah ruler (1921-59) and the man credited with a great deal of Kuwait's success and prosperity.

country, recognized today as one of the most progressive, moderate, literate, benevolent, and respected Arab nations in the world.

Although strong leadership has helped Kuwait mature, fate has certainly played a significant part in its history and success. On June 30, 1946, Sheikh Ahmad Al-Jaber Al-Sabah, the tenth Amir of Kuwait, slowly turned a silver handled valve at the site of today's Port Al-Ahmadi, and the precious oil from the Kuwaiti desert began to flow into the British tanker *Fusilier*.

It had been more than eight years since British drillers searching for oil in a remote location about 25 miles south of Kuwait City had first struck what Americans called "black gold." Oil had actually been discovered in Kuwait as early as 1934[8]. (See map on page xxvi.) However, it was the vast reserves of the Burgan Oil Field and the constantly improving export capability, that have served as the catalyst for Kuwait's economic restructuring. What was once an economy based upon harvest from the sea and merchant trade, has now become a society driven primarily by the quantity of oil pumped from the ground and shipped to the ravenous world energy market.

However, the Burgan discovery did not produce instant wealth for Kuwait and its people, but it was only a matter of time. Ultimately, Kuwait's oil reserves were confirmed as the third largest in the world, with only Saudi Arabia and the former Soviet Union having larger known reserves. Unfortunately, Kuwait had to be pa-

---

[8]   The first Middle East oil finds were in Iran (1908) and Iraq (1927). Kuwait's 1938 discovery in the Burgan Field was preceded by Bahrain (1932) and Saudi Arabia (1936). Qatar (1939), Abu Dhabi (1958) and Oman (1964) were next to locate Black Gold in their states. The world's first oil well was drilled near Titusville, Pennsylvania in 1859 by E. L. Drake. Most historians consider this United States' well to be the official beginning of the oil industry as we know it today.

tient because the task at hand in the 1930s was to develop the production and distribution infrastructure which was to enable Kuwait to move their "black gold" out of the ground and into the hands of consumers.

The combination of limited technology, extremely difficult desert working conditions, and the outbreak of World War II resulted in lengthy delays in establishing this critical infrastructure, thus explaining the eight-year delay from the initial Burgan discovery in 1938 until Kuwait was able to export its first shipment of crude in 1946. Great Britain's British Petroleum (BP) Company was the primary contributor to the early exploration and production of oil in Kuwait. BP was quickly joined, however, by the United States' Gulf Oil Corporation as well as oil companies from Holland, Japan, and Spain.

In 1980 Kuwait assumed total control of its oil industry by establishing the Kuwait Petroleum Corporation (KPC) to orchestrate the reorganization, integration and development of the country's entire oil sector. KPC is managed by a Board of Directors, which is currently chaired by the Kuwaiti's Minister of Oil. Today at full capacity, Kuwait's modern, sophisticated production system can extract and transport over 2.5 million barrels of crude oil each and every day.[9] Even at this impressive volume, estimates of Kuwait's known reserves indicate the oil will not be depleted for another 200 years. Economically speaking, the revenue generated from a single day of Kuwait oil production translates into over 40 million U.S. dollars.

In Kuwait, all of the mineral rights, including

---

[9] During the height of the OPEC production in the mid-seventies, Kuwait was substantially exceeding its design capacity by producing over 3 million barrels of oil per day. This extremely high production rate was maintained for less than two years.

petroleum and natural gas, are the property of the State of Kuwait. Income realized from the exploitation of those mineral rights is, therefore, retained for use by the State. Fortunately, for the people of Kuwait, the Al-Sabah Government has remained committed through the years to providing its people with all the benefits (discussed in detail in Chapter 6) associated with the country's considerable financial wealth.

Unlike Americans, many of whom complain that their income is reduced by as much as 50 percent because of the myriad of national, state, and local taxes, Kuwaitis pay no income taxes, no property taxes and no sales taxes. The only form of tax a Kuwaiti pays is toward a retirement system similar to America's Social Security System. But, because of huge revenue generated from the State owned mineral rights, all Kuwaiti residents (not just citizens) reap considerable free benefits: outstanding schools, excellent medical treatment, telephone service, parks, resorts and special care for the elderly. If you add to these advantages the heavily subsidized housing for Kuwaiti citizens and modern rental accommodations available, it becomes obvious why people from all over the world have gladly immigrated to this once unknown desert oasis.

The steady stream of immigrants and the fast-paced attempt at modernization has had a dramatic effect on Kuwait. Since Kuwait ended its status as a British Protectorate in 1961, the population has grown from about 330,000 to nearly 2.2 million. Before the mid-1970s, the distribution between Kuwaiti citizens and foreign residents was about equal, but in 1990 only 830,000 of the total residents of Kuwait were actually Kuwaiti citizens.

The almost uncontrolled influx of foreign residents to Kuwait eventually resulted in 139 different nationalities living and working in Kuwait prior to the Iraqi invasion, including 38 percent non-Kuwaiti Arabs and 21 percent Asians. The Kuwaitis had clearly become a minority in their own country. The impact of the Gulf War has resulted in approximately 600,000 fewer non-Kuwaiti citizens, making Kuwaitis a slight majority for the first time in many years.

Continuing to support the social structure and provide the countless benefits to the total population has begun to be a strain on the country's economy. The Government is currently investigating alternative methods such as user fees or surcharges for funding some of its social programs in order to offset the huge financial drain attributable to the disproportionate Kuwaiti-expatriate ratio.

History books are filled with accounts of nations who have achieved high levels of prosperity and power, only to fall gradually into ruin as a result of steadily declining moral values, continuous disregard for human needs, and the wanton misuse of the nation's natural and financial resources. History often lays the blame for this decay and decline at the feet of powerful leaders who realized great personal gain at the expense of the same people who had entrusted them with the sacred responsibility for determining the fate of the country and its people.

Kuwait's Al-Sabah family and the people who have empowered them to provide leadership since 1756 have enjoyed a peaceful, cooperative and prosperous relationship. With the exception of a potentially disastrous conspiracy to overthrow the Government in 1896 and an unsuccessful assassination attempt on His Highness the Amir in 1985, (terrorists from Iran and Iraq were suspected) there has been little evidence of serious discontent among the Kuwaiti people regarding the initiatives and policies undertaken by the long line of Al-Sabah leadership.

Actually, the 1896 incident resulted in the execution of Muhammad I, sixth Al-Sabah ruler and his brother Jaber, who was his designated successor, and marked the only deadly violence in the history of Kuwait's government. The executions did not involve the ordinary citizens of Kuwait, but was instead essentially a "family affair." Yusuf Ibrahim, an influential Kuwaiti merchant immigrant from that portion of the Ottoman Empire which was to eventually become modern Iraq, provided the motive for Mubarak Al- Sabah, Muhammad I's half brother, to plan and implement the executions.

Ibrahim's scheme was to remove Muhammad I as ruler and claim the lofty position for himself, thus ending not only the reign of the Al-Sabah family but also ending Kuwaiti control of Kuwait. Mubarak learned of the conspiracy and was certain his two half brothers would not have the courage to confront Ibrahim and put an end to the threat. Since Mubarak was already outraged with his restricted influence in the Kuwait government, he became convinced that he must take swift and decisive action for the sake of Kuwait and his family. He and his son, Jaber, carried out the murders, and Mubarak Al-Sabah became the seventh member of the Al-Sabah family to serve in the country's highest position of leadership.[10]

Under Mubarak's 20-year reign, Kuwait experienced an unprecedented growth and expanded prosperity. So successful and accepted was Mubarak, that Kuwait history books frequently refer to him as "Mubarak the Great," and all subsequent Kuwaiti rulers

---

[10] Al-Mubarak's son Jaber II succeeded his father as Amir (1915-1917) and his other son, Salim, succeeded Jaber (1917-1921).

descended from his blood line.

In recent years, and more noticeably since the Iraqi invasion, there have been calls for expanded democracy in Kuwait - - including the right to vote for women and increased freedom of speech and the press. Having faced most of the same issues in its early years, Americans can readily identify the challenges facing today's modern Kuwait.[11] In America we believe that people's personal needs and opinions must be respected. Likewise, Kuwaitis are beginning to understand that it is healthy to respectfully challenge the status quo; and, as the citizens of Kuwait become better educated and have greater exposure to other countries and cultures, they are motivated to refine and improve, although not necessarily to replace, the existing governmental process.

Perhaps the most reliable and meaningful measure of confidence and satisfaction with the existing government is the fact that the majority of Kuwaitis remain extremely loyal to the Al-Sabah family. Normal progress and political maturation will, undoubtedly, result in productive changes in Kuwait. But even those individuals most vocal in their criticism of the Royal Family will usually admit basic satisfaction with the leadership provided by the Al-Sabah government, and few would suggest ending their rule entirely.

Americans seeking to gain a realistic understanding of Kuwait, its people, and its culture must keep in mind at all times that Kuwait is an Islamic State.

This "marriage" of Church and State is a concept foreign to Americans and one that is hard to accept. The Constitution of the United States makes it abundantly

---

[11] It was 1920 (144 years after the Declaration of Independence) before the 19th Amendment to the Constitution was passed by the United States Congress and women were given the right to vote in political elections.

clear that in our country a distinct separation of Church and State shall be constantly maintained. The First Amendment to the Bill of Rights states, in part, "Congress shall make no law respecting an establishment of religion, or prohibiting the free exercise thereof; . . . " In contrast, Article 2 of the Constitution of the State of Kuwait reads, "The religion of the State is Islam, and the Islamic Sharia shall be the main source for legislation." In Kuwait there is no room for debate on this subject.

Although constitutionally mandated as the official religion, Islam is not overtly forced upon non-Muslims living in Kuwait. In fact, Article 36 of the Constitution of the State of Kuwait affirms that "Freedom of belief is absolute." Article 36 goes on to say, "The State protects the freedom of practicing religion in accordance with established customs, provided that it does not conflict with public policy or morals."

However, since the established customs, public policy, and morals of Kuwait are firmly founded on the Islamic religion, the potential for misunderstanding, disagreement, and drastically different interpretations of what is and is not allowed exists among the non-Muslim population. These matters of interpretation are especially sensitive in regard to the selection of clothing (how much of the body can be seen), as well as relations and communication with the opposite sex, drinking, eating, and smoking restrictions especially during specific Islamic religious periods; the most prohibitive of which is the month long period of fasting and sacrifice known as Ramadan.[12]

Despite what many visitors and "outsiders" may

---

[12] Ramadan is the ninth month in the Muslim year. It is the Islam's holy month of fasting and abstinence. Muslims may not eat or drink from dawn to sunset. The sick, nursing mothers and soldiers on the march are exempt, but must make up days missed.

consider unreasonable restrictions, Kuwait is actually one of the most tolerant of Arab countries in the area of religious freedom. Kuwait allows regular worship services for the country's non-Muslim contingent, which represented about five percent of the population, or over 100,000 people, prior to the Iraqi invasion.

Kuwait has earned the recognition as one of the most progressive and well-managed countries in the Middle East. In less than 30 years of existence as an independent nation, development has taken place at a break-neck pace. For example, only seventeen months elapsed from the day Kuwait declared its independence from Great Britain until His Highness the Amir of Kuwait officially ratified the State's first Constitution. Compared to the twelve years it took the founding fathers of the United States to accomplish the identical feat, Kuwait succeeded in record time and established a trend for its future endeavors.

Despite our obvious differences, a close look reveals that Kuwait and the United States, and our respective citizens, share many basic beliefs, ideals, morals, values and intellectual philosophies. The same close look also confirms that there are many areas of substantial difference between our two cultures. Kuwait is not America, and, not surprisingly, Kuwait does not aspire to become an American clone.

Americans, like the people of all other nations caught in this age of high technology and instant communication, must adapt to a world that is shrinking every day. In order to insure a peaceful and prosperous coexistence with our global neighbors in the years ahead, it is imperative that the culture, traditions, heritage, and aspirations of countries like Kuwait be investigated, understood and, perhaps most importantly, respected.[13]

---

[13] Kuwaitis in America want to be understood, accepted and respected. They are active members of the American Arab Anti-Discrimination Committee based in Washington, D.C. as well as the National Association of Arab Americans, which is an active group lobbying for more balanced U.S. policies in the Middle East. In May of 1991 the Kuwait-American Friendship Foundation was established to further improve relations between the two countries.

3

KUWAIT CITY

The Heart of a Proud Nation

Lee R. Lambert

*"The head learns new things, but the heart forever
more practices old experiences."*

Henry Ward Beecher

The April, 1986 timing for the Lambert family's
first visit to Kuwait City was not exactly optimum.
Several days before we were scheduled to depart Columbus, Ohio for Kuwait, the United States had unex-
pectedly launched an air attack on Libya as retaliation
for that country's alleged participation in deadly acts of
terrorism against American citizens abroad.

Almost simultaneously with the Cable News
Network (CNN) announcement of the Libyan attack,
our phone began to ring. Each call was from a friend or
relative, obviously in an intense emotional state, informing us of the new military action in the Middle East
region and, after adding reminders (described in vivid
detail) of the recent airline high-jackings and the
bloody airport attacks, begging us to cancel our
planned business trip to Kuwait City.

My first call to our State Department confirmed
that a Travel Advisory had, indeed, been issued for all
U.S. citizens, strongly suggesting that all but "absolutely necessary" travel to the region be avoided. My
next call was to Kuwait City and Dr. Abbas Alikhan,
Director for Symposia and Cultural Affairs of the Kuwait Foundation for the Advancement of Sciences

(KFAS), official sponsor of my trip. Dr. Abbas, without hesitation, provided assurances that the American attack upon Libya was having no impact on life in Kuwait City. He claimed that everything was "normal" and that my family should not worry, knowing that they would be perfectly safe in the quiet, friendly surroundings of Kuwait's capital city.

Dr. Abbas, through our cooperative business efforts in the U.S., had become my good friend, and I respected his advice. Against my wife, Carolyn's, better judgement then, and much to the astonishment of my friends and anxious relatives (who to this day attribute my actions to temporary insanity), I decided that the risk was minimal and that it was absolutely necessary for me to honor my contract to provide a management training seminar. The decision, having been made, Carolyn and I, together with our children, Marnie, Davin and Erin, (19, 16, and 13 years of age, respectively), admittedly still somewhat apprehensive, said good-bye to our friends and relatives and boarded a Delta Airlines' flight that Wednesday afternoon in April, 1986 en route to Kuwait City via Frankfurt, Germany.

Although our family had traveled extensively throughout the U.S., Canada, and Mexico, mostly by car, this was our first journey off the North American Continent. Even Carolyn, the consummate trip planner, who maintains files of meticulously "yellow highlighted" AAA and Fodor travel books, maps, reference material, and travel brochures, had found it frustratingly difficult to locate any substantive tourist-type information on Kuwait. Essentially, we embarked on our 7,000 mile trip to this tiny Arab country with almost no idea of what to expect when we arrived.

We did know the weather would be to our liking

- - very hot! We also had been assured that since English is Kuwait's unofficial second language, we should have no trouble communicating. These two facts, combined with Dr. Abbas' encouragement and the knowledge that we would be spending our free time in Kuwait City in the luxury of the seaside Regency Palace Hotel, allowed us to start the trip with a relatively positive attitude.

We were still thousands of miles away from Kuwait City when we began having second thoughts about our decision. Our flight plan called for a change from Delta to Lufthansa Airlines in Frankfurt. We stepped off the Delta plane directly onto what looked like the set for the latest Rambo movie.[14] Unfortunately, what we saw before us was not staged - - it was frighteningly real. Everywhere we looked we saw uniformed German soldiers brandishing automatic rifles over their shoulders and intimidating-looking 9mm pistols on their waists.

Security was unbelievably tight. In fact, the soldiers often outnumbered the passengers in the Frankfurt airport terminal. Everyone was a suspect, and even we (unlikely terrorists) were subjected to two "patdown" searches. Naturally, our carry-on luggage was completely unpacked and every item carefully inspected. Once security was satisfied, several hours remained before our plane was to depart for Kuwait City, so we began wandering around the airport. We quickly noticed that the majority of waiting passengers were of Arab nationality and that everyone (at least it seemed like everyone) was staring and pointing at us. Although we had no idea as to what was being said, we were

---

[14]   Rambo is a famous American movie character portrayed by actor Silvester Stallone. Rambo movies involve extensive use of weapons and violence as the lead character overcomes tremendous odds to defeat the villains.

convinced that most of the conversation and laughter was targeted at us as well. As we glanced around the crowded terminal, it became painfully obvious we were the only Americans. For the first time in our lives, we experienced how threatening and lonely it is to be among the minority in a strange place.

Our imaginations soon began to run wild, and it wasn't long before visions of kidnapping and murder at the hands of some enraged Libyan or other anti-American terrorist swirled through our minds. Frankly, we were worried and scared. It was the same fear of the unknown we had experienced the first time we walked alone down a dark back street in New York City. Without hesitation, we decided to find a quiet, isolated spot where we could wait inconspicuously for our flight to Kuwait City.

The hours passed slowly, but finally we were through the gate and aboard the majestic Boeing 747 which would carry us to our final destination. It was comforting to know we could count on American technology no matter where we were in the world. The flight attendant began a rapid-fire series of announcements. First in German, then in Arabic, and finally, much to our relief, in English, she extended a warm Lufthansa welcome, instructed everyone on the use of the safety equipment and provided our estimated time of arrival in Kuwait City - - 7:30 p.m., Thursday. Including the eight hours lost in time zone changes, we would touch down at Kuwait International Airport about 30 hours from the time we left Columbus, Ohio.

I settled into my seat and was just nodding off for a power nap when I heard a low-pitched, constant "Hmmmm, Hmmmmmmmm, Hmmmmm" coming from the person seated to my immediate right. I slowly turned my head in that direction and lifted my eyelid just enough to get a peek at my neighbor. What I saw was a very lean young man, I guessed about 25 years old, sitting cross-legged, rocking slowly forward and back, forward and back, as he chanted, "Hmmm, Hmmmmmm, Hmmmmm."

Carolyn thought my seat-mate might be from India. Based on what I saw and heard, I was inclined to believe he was from "another world." I was convinced of it when our meals arrived and the young man pushed back the sleeves on his white "nightshirt" and proceeded to devour his food without even a thought of using a fork or spoon. He simply filled both of his hands with rice and vegetables and began stuffing them into his mouth. A good quantity of the rice fell short of his mouth, coming to rest in and among the bristles of his beard. Within seconds his food had disappeared and the resonating sound of "Hmmmmm, Hmmm, Hmmmmm" once again filled my ears. I looked around the plane's cabin to see if everyone was as astonished by this young man's actions as I. No one else seemed to notice. I wondered silently, "Is this young man a sample of what Dr. Abbas had described as "normal" in Kuwait?" I forced myself to go back to sleep, secretly hoping I would awake in Kuwait City and learn it had all been a dream.

The screeching sound of rubber meeting the runway pavement brought me out of a deep sleep. My eyes quickly focused on the seat to my right - - it hadn't been a dream. The young man was for real. I was relieved to learn he was continuing his trip to New Delhi and that he was not Kuwaiti. I quickly put the unusual experience out of my mind. We were safely on the ground in Kuwait, and I couldn't wait to get my first glimpse of the city that would be our home for the next ten days.

As we left the plane and entered the terminal, we

saw a sample of the architecture we could expect when we reached downtown Kuwait City. The building was spacious, over two stories high, with very wide, polished marble tile walkways. Concrete appeared to be the building material of choice as cold, gray walls stretched almost as far as the eye could see. Large panes of glass, strategically placed, divided the main floor of the terminal into sections for incoming and outgoing passengers. It is a large airport, and as we followed the dual-language signs (Arabic & English) to Immigration on the lower level, we quickly observed that it is also a very busy airport. Literally thousands of people, dressed in the most outrageous clothes we had ever seen, were jammed into nearly every available open space.

We learned later that our arrival had unfortunately coincided with the end of Kuwait's version of the U.S. "spring break" holiday. The airport crowd, considerably less obnoxious and obviously much less "hungover" than the U.S. spring break veterans we had observed in Ohio returning from a week of non-stop parties in Ft. Lauderdale, Florida, grew even larger as anxious friends and relatives formed a huge welcome-home contingent.

Thoroughly exhausted from our trip and a long delay in obtaining our visas, we claimed our bags, cleared Kuwait Customs, and gladly settled into our KFAS arranged car and departed Kuwait International Airport for downtown Kuwait City. (See map page xxvii.) The excitement of knowing we were finally in Kuwait City gave us a burst of energy. It was nearly midnight, but we were wide-eyed as we left the airport. Even the extreme heat, which saw temperatures hovering near 100° F. as we left the efficiently air-conditioned terminal, couldn't dampen our enthusiasm for what we would see in the days ahead. Our car merged onto a brightly lit, four lane highway that would earn some respect from even the harried commuters of Los Angeles. Thousands of city lights on the northern horizon twinkled an imaginary "welcome - - welcome" to the first-time visitors from America. Thirty minutes later we had completed the check-in process at the Regency Palace Hotel and were comfortably resting in our beds.

The next morning, our first daylight glimpse of Kuwait City was truly breathtaking. We arose to the bright sunshine we had expected; however, as we looked out from our hotel room window toward the east, we received our first of many pleasant surprises - a 180° view of the Arabian Gulf. During our stay we spent many hours in front of this window, our attention alternating between the hotel's clear, fresh-water pool surrounded by palm trees and a carpet of well-groomed, deep green lawn, and the calm, essentially boat-less expanse of a sea that rippled gently onto the shore just yards away.[15] We have visited some of the finest vacation resorts in America, and none can surpass the beauty and tranquility we discovered at our oasis in the Kuwait desert.

Traveling in our car north from our hotel along the sea front, it was obvious that the metropolitan area most people refer to as Kuwait City was a modern, thriving community. Streets were lined with businesses and residential developments. Auto and foot traffic was extremely heavy as throngs of people from 139 different nations criss-crossed the streets and filled the sidewalks as they went about their daily work or household

---

[15] Prior to the 1980s Iran-Iraq war the Arabian Gulf waters were filled with fishing and pleasure boats. However, due to the extensive placement of mines in Gulf waters, almost all boating activity was terminated.

responsibilities. For miles the shoreline was filled with fishermen, each sporting a fishing rod at least twelve feet long and large enough in diameter to be used for catching the biggest deep sea fish. The sight leaves the impression that fishing from the shore in the Gulf must be quite rewarding; however, as many times as I have visited Kuwait, I have yet to see a single one of these fishermen catch a fish.

Although the number of people and level of activity was eye catching, perhaps the two most immediately noticeable sights for the first time visitor to Kuwait City were sand, everywhere you looked and for as far as you could see, and the mosques with their minarets (towers from which people are called to prayer) reaching high into the sky. These beautiful and functional structures could be seen in a wide variety of architectural forms scattered generously throughout the city. The mosques provide permanent locations for Muslims to pray; and often, following completion of prayers, large groups of people remain outside the mosque, mixing and socializing with friends and relatives.

The area originally known as Kuwait City, which is the seat of the government and the National Assembly, is a very small parcel of land consisting of approximately 2,000 acres, or one-tenth the land mass of Manhattan Island, New York. However, it is this tiny historic section on the northern-most tip of Kuwait - - which from 1760 until 1957 was protected from attack by first one and finally three simple mud walls[16] - - that supplies the lifeblood to this thriving country. In addi-

---

[16] The Arab name for the mud walls is "Sour." Although the *sours* were destroyed in 1957, five gates were preserved. One of these gates was demolished by Iraqi troops. Damage to the gates will be repaired.

tion to government offices, the high-rise main offices of most banks and investment firms, major hospitals, and the Kuwait National Museum and the Amir's Seif Palace are all situated within this small land mass.

Once in the original Kuwait City, you can't miss the world famous Kuwait Towers.[17] This prominent landmark is 160 feet high and is strategically located at the point where Kuwait juts farthest into the Arabian Gulf. Admittedly small in comparison to the Statue of Liberty, Seattle's Space Needle, or the Washington Monument (305, 607, and 555 feet high, respectively) the Kuwait Towers, built in 1979, have become the world's most recognized symbol of this tiny country. Kuwaitis appreciate the beauty of Kuwait Towers, but are quick to point out that they have a vital functional purpose as well. Two of the three bright blue towers are operating water reservoirs with a combined capacity of one-and-a-half million gallons of fresh, pure water. The Kuwait Towers are by far the most visible water reservoir tanks in Kuwait City, but dozens of others, attractively painted but less spectacular, can be seen throughout the city as precious water is stored to insure a constant supply for residents.

In addition to their primary function of water storage, the Kuwait Towers is also a favorite tourist attraction, providing a breathtaking view of Kuwait City from the observation deck of the largest tower's rotating restaurant, 132 feet above ground. The smallest of the towers is "sphereless," but also has an important function - - showering its larger counterparts with bright light, making them visible from miles away on a

---

[17]   The National Museum, Seif Palace and the Kuwait Towers all were heavily damaged during the Iraqi occupation. As of May 1992 all were under repair.

clear night.

Not far from the Kuwait Towers, located in the heart of the city's commercial center, is the nearly completed Kuwait Communication Center Tower. This impressive structure rises 405 feet above ground and, when finished in approximately 1993, will be the fourth highest tower of its kind in the world and home to Kuwait's third (the other is atop the Al-Sharq Tower office building) rotating restaurant (few American cities can boast one). The restaurant and its observation platform will provide visitors with a commanding view of Kuwait City and the Arabian Gulf from an elevation of 160 feet.

Approximately four miles west of the Kuwait Towers is one of Kuwait City's well planned industrial sites. The Shuwaikh Industrial Area provides working space for car dealers, warehouses, transportation terminals, and assorted light industrial ventures. The Shuwaikh Port, one of the finest deep-water shipping ports in the Gulf, is also considered a part of this thriving business complex. The vast number of workers who commute to this busy area during rush hour often results in grid-lock traffic jams that remind me of my commuting experiences on the highways around Oakland and San Francisco, California, in the late 1960s and early 1970s.

At the center of the Shuwaikh Industrial Area, near the sea, are the campuses of Kuwait University and the Kuwait Applied Technology College (see Chapter 8 for additional details). When these schools are in session, over 20,000 students, both male and female, join the industrial-area workers on the already crowded inner-city blacktop arteries.

Fortunately, for those faced with the task of frequent driving, Kuwait officials have recognized the traffic problems that accompany rapid urbanization and are planning and implementing approaches to reduce the impact as quickly as possible. In 1977 only a few paved roads existed. Today over 2,500 miles of finished roadways are in use, with nearly 200 miles of those being major expressways equal or superior to many in the United States. The majority of Kuwait's expressway-quality highways are part of the elaborate and efficient "ring-road" system in which inner-city roads connect with inter-suburban roads which are radial, forming a series of seven semi-circles fanning out from the center of Kuwait City for approximately ten miles to the south, just beyond Kuwait International Airport.[18] Kuwait's ring-road concept is similar to America's interstate by-pass system, which allows travelers using highways encircling most major cities to reach destinations quickly throughout the city without having to traverse the congested inner-city roadway system.

Once you become familiar with the ring-road concept and the general layout of Kuwait City, it is surprisingly easy, fast and convenient to travel by car (auto travel in Kuwait is not necessarily the safest in the world - - see Chapter 12). Wisely, Kuwait avoided the influence of its long-time friend and supporter Great Britain and designed its road system for American style cars, built for driving on the "right" side of the road. No one I asked could recall when they decided to drive on the right. Most of the people responded, "It's just the way we always have." Although driving in Kuwait's environment of high speeds and sometimes wanton

---

[18] It was from an apartment location near the 7th Ring Road that an American basketball coach living in Kuwait was among the first to report the sighting of approaching Iraqi tanks and soldiers.

disregard for traffic laws is clearly not for the weak-hearted or timid, eventually, with a little practice, even the challenge of conquering the hazardous Kuwait City "roundabouts" becomes no more intimidating than facing the same difficult assignment on Boston's legendary traffic circles.

Whether you drive or choose some other form of transportation, the sights awaiting you in Kuwait City will provide memories that last a lifetime. Traveling through the city streets along the luxurious Water Front Project, with its miles of wide brick walkways and lush green landscaping, you immediately notice the contrasting blend of old and new. Modern high rise banks and office buildings, some towering over twenty stories, cast their shadows on traditional single-story mud structures that have been home to Kuwaiti merchant and sea-faring families for two centuries.

Since the discovery of significant oil reserves in 1938, the growth and modernization of Kuwait has progressed at a breakneck pace. Fortunately, a Kuwait Master Plan has been carefully developed and includes cultural and informational provisions and organizations and facilities dedicated to preserving and protecting the history and culture that forms a solid foundation for Kuwait's future. An excellent example of this dedication to preserving Kuwait's heritage is the five huge wooden gates that once provided the only inland access to the original Kuwait City through three separate, semi-circular walls. Although the last of the walls was removed in 1957, the massive gates were left intact as monuments providing the people with a constant reminder of their past.

Eventually, as a new generation of Kuwaiti is born, and more and more choose to leave the ways of the past for the conveniences of the future, the old traditional mud structures are razed, and new modern buildings take their place. However, the government has assured those who desire to hold onto the past that they will not be forced to relocate in the interest of modernization and, in many cases, the government is preserving traditional structures as historical museums.

More evidence of Kuwait's attention to maintaining the memory of its past can be seen and actually experienced by visitors who take part in one of the Kuwaiti's favorite activities - - shopping! Kuwait's old *souk* (market), located close to the waterfront near the Amir's Seif Palace, has been preserved and restored to reflect the traditional Kuwaiti approach to shopping. Small, independently owned shops on both sides of the street as well as large, open-air buildings off the street, house merchants selling every imaginable product. Each merchant usually has a specialty item, and the salesmen are willing and eager to barter aggressively on the selling price. There is a *souk* just for watches, as well as individual souks for rugs, luggage, fabrics, electronics, clothing, shoes and, of course, every American visitor's favorite - - gold!

It is an overwhelming first-time experience to see store after store, window after window, filled with beautiful, gleaming gold hammered into all shapes and sizes. During just one trip to the gold *souk,* you will see more of the ageless, precious metal than most people will see in a lifetime. The workmanship is excellent, the gold is extremely high in quality (usually 22 or 24 karat), and the prices irresistibly low. The first time I worked in Kuwait I was convinced there was a conspiracy between my employer and the gold *souk*. I was paid my fee on the final day of my assignment and was advised that a trip to the gold *souk* had been arranged for the following morning! This journey to the gold *souk* has now become mandatory on each of our visits, at least as far as Carolyn is concerned. She takes great pride in the gold pieces she has acquired and she will gladly tell the story behind each one.

No trip to the old *souk* would be complete without wandering into some of the out-of-the-way alleys where you can find great deals on "Rolex" and "Gucci" watches. It's not Fifth Avenue or Central Park in New York, but the watches are just as phony, the sales pitch is suspiciously the same and, coincidentally, so is the price, about 10 Kuwaiti Dinar (US $34). In the typical friendly Kuwaiti merchants tradition, by our third trip to Kuwait these fake watch merchants recognized our family and knew what we liked. This unique Kuwaiti merchant dedication to extending his customers the utmost hospitality is best illustrated by the dozens of immigrant workers who are hired to constantly serve coffee,[19] tea or bottled water to the thirsty shoppers.

On Thursday, Kuwait's equivalent of Saturday in the U.S., all of the old *souk* shops are filled beyond capacity as Kuwaitis and foreign residents alike attempt to out-shop each other. You quickly notice that the most aggressive, and, perhaps the most successful shoppers are the local Bedouin women, old and young alike. These ladies, clothed in heat-absorbing black from head to toe, their faces either completely covered or penetrating dark eyes barely visible, and each arm

---

[19] Coffee is the translation of the Arabic word "qahwah." Coffee is a very popular drink in Kuwait and it is a symbol of hospitality. Legend indicates coffee was first discovered by an Arab goatherder when his flock began acting strangely after eating from a wild coffee bush. As a stimulant, coffee was said to be against the teachings of the Koran and banned. However, coffee's popularity has grown rapidly and today it is no longer challenged on religious grounds.

displaying dozens of beautiful gold bangles, just won't take "no" for an answer, and, eventually, even the most stubborn shopkeeper relents.

It is a must to visit the old *souk*, but, if possible, attempt to time your trip to avoid Thursday. The best time to shop is in the evening when the hot sun has disappeared and the crowds have diminished. One warning, the old *souk* does not have dual language signs. At the old *souk* it is "Arabic only."

Carolyn and I learned this lesson the hard way. It was our first unaccompanied visit to the *souk*. After nearly an hour of searching for a space, I had finally parked our rental car on the street in the late afternoon, and we leisurely wandered through the *souk*, admiring the items for sale and occasionally buying some things to take back to America as gifts. By the time we completed our shopping, darkness had set in. As we looked around to find our car, it didn't take long to realize that we had absolutely no idea where we had parked. To us, all the signs read the same, all the buildings looked identical, and even the cars all looked alike. At first we weren't worried, but after almost an hour of wandering helplessly, searching for our car among hundreds lining the streets, we became concerned. Since we had no idea where the car was, or for that matter where we were, we couldn't even ask for directions. It was very late and panic set in. I imagined us, days later, still searching for the car. I was just looking for a phone to call my good friend Adnan Al-Abdulmuhsen to come to our rescue when I recognized the vacant lot we had walked through on our way to the old *souk*. We retraced our steps and within minutes were standing, relieved, beside our rental car.

Less adventurous shoppers may choose to spend their time in Kuwait City's modern shopping areas, which more closely resemble the malls, department stores, and arcades found in America. The Salhia Complex provides a venue for the "upscale," sophisticated, one-stop shopper. This three-level, marble-floored arcade provides a stylish shopping atmosphere in the image of a small Trump Tower in New York or the Galleria in Houston. The complex, located behind the downtown Le Meridien Hotel, boasts some of the finest brand names in the world. One of the names familiar to the wealthy American shoppers would be Van Cleef & Arpel, a high-priced custom jewelry distributor, which operates from a prime location on world-renown Rodeo Drive in Beverly Hills, California. Other brands easily recognized by Americans visiting Kuwait include Gucci, Salvadore Ferragamo, Valentino, Cartier, Yves St. Laurent, Ralph Lauren and Charles Jordan.

Only a few minutes drive from the center of Kuwait City is another option for local shoppers - - Al-Khaleejia, Kuwait's first attempt at a luxury, European-style department store, and the first of its kind anywhere in the Gulf.[20]

The more traditional American shopper may prefer the familiarity of Kuwait's version of the popular U.S. "strip shopping." In this regard, Kuwait once again offers both the old and new. The "new strip," as it is familiarly called in Kuwait, is located on Salem Al-Mobarak Street in the suburb of Salmiya. Nearly any product that comes to an American's mind may be purchased, but be prepared to pay a premium price. Since its conversion into a quasi-pedestrian precinct in 1982, this Salmiya location has become a favorite shopping

---

[20] Al-Khaleejia opened in 1984, but the European-style experiment failed. It closed its doors after only several years, and was converted to a popular mini-mall offering a variety of shops and an amusement arcade.

hangout for the younger set. On weekends and most evenings, Salmiya is transformed from a shopping strip to an "auto drag strip,"[21] as a steady stream of cars and the popular small pick-up trucks constantly drive up and down the street, stereos blasting American and Arabic music (heavy on the bass), with passengers hanging out the windows, calling out to old friends and frequently stopping to make new acquaintances. Our daughters, Marnie and Erin, got to experience for themselves just how friendly the "boys" in Kuwait can be. They were walking along the street in Salmiya with their friend, Khaloud, when a truck full of young men began whistling and yelling to attract their attention. The encounter reminded them of similar occasions in America, but, before they could return the greetings, Khaloud warned them that due to religious beliefs in Kuwait such attempts to be friendly by the opposite sex are to be ignored. So, the girls quickly darted into a Pizza Hut to avoid drawing any more attention.

The first commercial shopping spot in Kuwait, the "old strip," was established in central Kuwait city over 20 years ago. Until the mid-1970s the Fahd Al-Salem Street shopping was the city's most popular. Although many of the shops seem outdated today in comparison to the new stylish centers, and most have begun to show their age, Fahd Al-Salem Street remains a thriving commercial area with an excellent variety of goods at prices considerably lower than the high-over-head competition in the Salmiya district.

Actually, shopping in Kuwait City is almost like

---

[21] These "auto drag strips" have long been the center of a social phenomena in America. Young adults spend countless evening hours in their cars driving back and forth on popular thoroughfares such as Sunset Strip in Hollywood, California. Nearly every American city has its "strip" and it is always filled with drivers and passengers looking for a good time.

shopping in your hometown in America. Groceries could be purchased at the familiar Safeway supermarket, one of the largest of its kind in the world. Children could keep up with the latest fads in games and toys with a quick trip to Toys 'R Us next door to the Safeway.[22] At the end of a tough day of Kuwait City shopping you will want something to eat and in true American fashion, you want it fast. You're in luck. There is a full assortment of familiar American-style fast food outlets and pizza parlors, including Kentucky Fried Chicken, Baskin-Robins 31 Ice Cream, Pizza Hut and Hardees. Kuwait is one of the few developed countries in the world where you will not be able to purchase a McDonald's Big Mac.[23]

Once we had visited the various shopping hot spots, and had seen the university and the planned industrial site, the most enjoyable part of our on-going Kuwait City tour came next - - a visit to the suburbs and an opportunity to see some of the beautiful residential developments that have accompanied rapid growth and financial prosperity. Masterfully planned, Kuwait City's metropolitan area comprises a group of semi-self-sustaining districts, or as Americans call them, "suburbs," neatly divided by the ring-road system. (See map page xxvii.) Finding your way to a particular suburb is not too difficult; however, once you are in the suburb, finding a specific house can be almost impossible. The house numbering system is practically non-

---

[22] Both of these popular stores were completely looted and burned during the Iraqi occupation. The elaborate Sultan Center and an abundance of elaborate neighborhood co-ops provide Kuwaitis numerous options as replacements for the destroyed stores.

[23] McDonald's is interested in the Arab market, however, concerns regarding potential modifications to McDonald's strict food preparation processes and procedures have thus far prevented an agreement that would bring Big Mac to Kuwait.

existent, and most of the housing areas look very much the same. Even taxi drivers have a difficult time locating a house if you can not provide comprehensive information about landmarks or buildings.

Once in the residential areas, few commercial buildings exist. The only significant exception in this regard is the Bayan Palace, the site of the Fifth Islamic Summit Conference hosted by Kuwait in 1986. This huge self-contained conference center is located on the Fifth Ring Road near the suburb of Jabriya. The facility was built specifically for the Fifth Islamic Summit Conference and was completed in less than two years. The complex, which includes housing for hundreds of delegates, one of the largest auditoriums in the world, and beautifully landscaped grounds, complete with fountains and ponds, was opened briefly for public tours following conclusion of the Islamic Summit. All those lucky enough to visit Bayon Palace, including Carolyn, admit without reservation that they have never seen anything that survives comparison.

Carolyn, Erin and Davin had similar feelings of being overwhelmed by the beauty and history they saw on their private tour of the Kuwait National Museum. Ghada Hijjawi Qaddumi, the Museum Curator and our friend Nabil Qaddumi's mother, personally escorted them through one of the finest collections of Islamic art in the world. They learned that the art of the Muslim people is an integral part of their total Islamic culture.

The new Kuwait National Museum building, located in Kuwait City between the Amir's Seif Palace and the new National Assembly Building on Arabian Gulf Street, has been open since 1983 and is the home to the Dar Al-Athar Al-Islamiyyah (The Museum of Islamic Art) and the personal collection of Sheikh Nasser Sabah Al-Ahmed Al-Sabah, nephew of the current Amir, and his wife, Sheikha Hussa Sabah Al-Salem Al-Sabah, the daughter of a former Amir. Because their personal collection had become so large (at last count over 20,000 pieces), and because they have such a strong desire to allow others to enjoy this incredible assemblage of precious Islamic art, they provided the entire collection as a permanent loan to the Kuwait National Museum.

Sadly, the invading Iraqi army looted the Kuwait National Museum of most of the collections and destroyed or vandalized those pieces they chose not to pack and ship to Baghdad. The Great Dhow,[24] which had become a landmark of the Kuwait National Museum, was burned by Iraqi vandals until all that remained was the metal anchor and a huge pile of ashes. However, since the end of the Iraqi occupation, it has been reported that the majority of the items taken from the Museum have been found intact and returned to Kuwait.[25]

The return of this collection to Kuwait City is viewed as a very significant event for Muslims everywhere but especially for Kuwaitis. The collection dates as far back as the eighth century and includes pottery, jewelry, textiles, coins, manuscripts, and wood carvings. Carolyn, Erin and Davin have such vivid memories that when they learned of the Iraqi looting, they felt almost as saddened as the Kuwaitis themselves.

Kuwait houses must be seen to be believed. As we were driven around the suburbs on our first visit to Kuwait City, we assumed that the rows of buildings we drove past must be small to medium-sized office complexes. A few days later we learned that the two-and

---

[24] A *dhow* is a ship with lateen (triangular) sails used primarily along the coasts of Arabia, India and eastern Africa.

[25] The precious art collection is in storage awaiting repairs to the National Museum.

three-story, ornately appointed buildings weren't offices at all, these were the homes of typical suburban Kuwaiti citizens and their families.

At first glance, many of the homes look very similar from the street. Each has a large rooftop water tank and most have a series of unsightly television antennas or an oversized satellite dish.[26] Usually built in a large square or rectangle, using a combination of stone and concrete, each owner adds personal touches with the use of uniquely shaped windows, fancy "gingerbread," and eye-catching entry ways. Although a variety of exterior colors can be found, the Kuwaiti home colors of choice seem to be white or light grey, both of which are aesthetically pleasing and functionally efficient as a reflector of the desert sun's constant and intense heat. As in America, deviations from the norm can be found but not frequently. For example, my family has been entertained in a 10,000 square foot, completely round house, and we have visited a home with so many wings it could have served as a small apartment complex, but these are structural exceptions.

Once inside the house, however, the huge rooms (300 to 400 square feet each with 10-foot ceilings) quickly take on the personality, warmth and charm of its owners. Mementos of travel throughout the world typically decorate each room, and the gracious Kuwaiti hosts will gladly take time to tell the interesting history of each item. The houses are very spacious (five to six thousand feet is common) with five or more bedrooms to accommodate the large Kuwaiti families, which can sometimes include grown children, grandparents, and aunts and uncles, as well as the core family unit.

---

[26] Ninety-nine percent of all Kuwaiti electrical and telephone service is underground

Basically, the Kuwaiti home has the same complement of rooms as the modern home in America, including a large informal room for socializing (family room) and a formal room for entertaining (living room). Often, however, you will find two kitchens serving the Kuwaiti household. The "inside" kitchen is used for preparation and light meals, while the "outside" kitchen is primarily for cooking and baking. This arrangement, which has been common through many generations of Kuwaitis, allows the meals to be cooked away from the view of the family guests and prevents strong cooking odors and heat from invading the main portion of the house. For those not fortunate enough to have a separate cooking kitchen, most neighborhoods have small shops that specialize in preparing main dishes to each customer's precise specifications, especially the delicious, but strong-smelling fish, which can be purchased within hours of being caught by visiting the Gulf Street commercial fish market.

These small, one-man cooking shops have been opened by ambitious immigrants who want to own their business and provide a valuable service to Kuwaitis and other immigrants alike. A friend introduced me to this convenient approach to dinner preparation one day after a trip to the fish market. He had selected his fish, and we promptly drove to a small shop two blocks from his house where the cook was awaiting his arrival. My friend gave him the fish and told him what spices he preferred, and we left for his house. About an hour later, a phone call confirmed that dinner was ready and we made the pick-up. It was great! No fish cleaning, no cooking, no odors, and no mess. These small shops have become an important element of every Kuwaiti residential community, whether it is an old development or one of the many new housing areas currently being built.

Everywhere you look, evidence can be seen of the enormous amount of energy and resources being targeted at meeting the housing needs of the Kuwaiti people. Individual housing units and multi-unit, single family dwellings dot the landscape, each in various stages of completion, with some anxious soon-to-be Kuwaiti owners having waited up to 10 years for their names to reach the top of the housing allocation list. Severe working conditions, difficulty in obtaining adequate supplies of building materials, restrictions on land use, and simple economics result in long waits for home ownership. After seeing the size and versatility of the homes in Kuwait, I am convinced that the wait may be worth it.

Kuwait City is a unique and exciting melting pot of people and traditions from throughout the world. Prior to the Iraqi invasion in 1990, nearly 75 percent of the country's nearly 2.2 million residents lived in the Kuwait City metropolitan area, including all of the surrounding suburbs. This pre-war population figure makes Kuwait City comparable in size to such well known U.S. cities as Milwaukee, San Francisco, Kansas City, and San Jose. All one million-and-a-half residents of Kuwait City are concentrated in an area which represents only about ten percent of Kuwait's total territory.

The only other significant population center in Kuwait is Ahmadi City, the headquarters for most of the country's oil operations, and its surrounding suburbs. An estimated 300,000 people, a large proportion being foreigners working in the oil industry, reside in this growing area some 26 miles due east from downtown Kuwait City. A third city, Jahra, is expected to become a new growth area in the years ahead. Known as the agricultural city of Kuwait, Jahra, situated less than 20 miles south and west of Kuwait's capital, has already begun to expand rapidly with the construction of modern houses and commercial buildings in and around the city.

Hopefully, I have been able to provide a representative overview of what I think makes Kuwait City so important and such an enjoyable place to visit. No matter how many times I go to Kuwait City, no matter how long I stay, each new day seems to bring another opportunity for gaining new experiences, making new friends and obtaining a much better understanding of why Kuwait and its proud heritage have managed to survive since the early 1700s. Kuwait City has passed the test of time. Kuwait City retains and sustains its people's traditions. Kuwait City holds the key to the "door of knowledge" about Kuwait. Unlock it and behold the wonders before your eyes.

4

THE PEOPLE OF KUWAIT

Its Most Valuable Asset

Lee R. Lambert

*"Other lands have had their vitality in a few, a class,
but we have it in the bulk of our people."*

Walt Whitman

Kuwait and oil. These two words are nearly synonymous to people throughout the world. Fate has been good to this tiny Middle East nation. It has been blessed with the world's third largest quantity of oil or "black gold," one of the most valuable natural resources known to man.

Yet, this underground reservoir of seemingly endless "liquid assets" takes a distant second when we identify the key factor that makes Kuwait one of the most stimulating, enjoyable, and memorable places that I have ever had the opportunity to visit. What makes Kuwait so unique? Easy answer: The Kuwaiti people! Without a doubt, it is the people!

If someone had asked me about the people of Kuwait an hour after the Lambert family landed at Kuwait International Airport in April 1986, my assessment would have been substantially different. In fact, I might have suggested that the people of Kuwait were insensitive, perhaps even rude. Such a snap judgement would have illustrated in a dramatic way how dangerous and inaccurate it is to draw conclusions and form strong opinions based on limited exposure and first impressions.

Remember, my only contact with the people of Kuwait up to that point had been in a strictly business environment on my "turf." I had taught a management training seminar for 20 Kuwaiti men in Seattle in 1983 and had organized and taught in the 1985 Kuwait Foundation for the Advancement of Sciences (KFAS) Overseas Program in San Francisco, where I met another 40 Kuwaiti business executives. We got along very well. We all wore conservative business suits. We all spoke English. And, we all possessed and enjoyed an imaginative sense of humor. Except for the Arab accents, abstention from the use of alcohol and five breaks a day for prayer, these men could easily have been the average American next door instead of visitors from thousands of miles away.

With that background, then you can imagine my surprise upon landing in Kuwait when it took over an hour and several telephone calls to convince the Kuwaiti Immigration Officer to give us our visas. (I've since learned that significant delays in obtaining your "preapproved" visa clearly fits into Dr. Abbas' original description of "normal" in Kuwait.) Finally, we exited the Immigration security doors and marched down the path leading to baggage claim as hundreds of people, staring in search of their returning loved ones, began to notice the Lambert family. I tried to avoid staring back, but it was impossible not to hear the whispers, giggles, and an occasional belly laugh.

The more I thought about it, the more upset I became. After all, we were Americans. We were the ones who should have been laughing. Not a single person in this crowd of anxious onlookers looked "normal" to me. As a matter of fact, they didn't look anything like the Kuwaitis I had worked with in Seattle and San Francisco! No one had on a business suit. In fact, very

few even wore slacks and a sport shirt. Almost every-
one, men and women alike, wore floor-length gowns
that bore a striking resemblance to the nightshirt
Ebenezer Scrooge wore when he was visited by the
Ghosts of Christmas in the famous story "A Christmas
Carol."

We felt very uncomfortable being the center of so
much attention, so we quickly collected our bags and
urged our KFAS driver, who we were pleased to see had
dressed "correctly" in pants and a short-sleeved shirt, to
take us to the hotel. As we entered the spacious, three-
story-high lobby of the Regency Palace Hotel, it was
more of the same - - dozens of people milling about in
their strange-looking clothes. All eyes turned our way
as I provided the registration information, and we departed for our assigned suite.

Once behind the privacy of closed doors, we
paused silently, individually reflecting on what had
just happened. We looked at one another inquisitively.
Each pair of Lambert eyes scanned the other members
of the family from head to toe in order to determine the
cause of all this unwelcome attention. Everything was
in perfect order. We had worn our best Ralph Lauren
Polo resort wear to be sure we made a good impression
in our new surroundings: powder blue, pink, yellow
and green shirts and blouses with color coordinated
shorts and shoes. These same sporty clothes had been a
big hit in hot sun-sand-and-sea destinations like California, Hilton Head, Hawaii, Mexico and Florida. We
had been told it would be hotter in Kuwait, and we had
come prepared. Our plan was to soak up the sun's rays,
while achieving our goal of being the "coolest" Americans in Kuwait.

Almost simultaneously, after one last look, we
all burst into laughter. What a sight we must have been

to the native Arabs at the airport. Surely, they had all seen Americans before, but we could be certain they had never seen any as conspicuous. We must have looked like a walking rainbow, but instead of a pot of gold, only a huge stack of luggage was waiting at the end - - luggage filled with mostly more of the same colorful, trendy, inappropriate clothes.

The next morning when our good friend Adnan Al-Abdulmuhsen arrived at the hotel, we could not wait to tell him about our airport experience. Anxious to see a familiar face, we rushed to the lobby to meet him. We kept looking, but Adnan was nowhere in sight. Suddenly it dawned on me that Adnan would probably be wearing one of those nightshirts (*dishdasha*)[27] we had seen the night before. Fortunately, Adnan, in his crisply pressed, snow-white *dishdasha*, equally white head dress cloth (*gatra*), and cord circlet (*agal*) found us, and our eight-month wait to be reunited following the San Francisco seminar was over.

We said our hellos and reconstructed for Adnan our embarrassing airport story. Like most Kuwaitis, Adnan tried to be extremely diplomatic about our ordeal, but eventually, as he painted his mental image of the "walking rainbow" he could not hide a big smile. Adnan tried to make us feel better by taking responsibility for our discomfort and sincerely apologizing for not better preparing us for the drastic differences in Kuwait and American clothing styles. But, frankly, we had no one to blame but ourselves. A few simple telephone calls would have enlightened us; not only are bright, flashy-colored clothes inappropriate, but wearing shorts of any kind, especially for women, is not

---

[27] A *dishdasha* is a basic long-sleeved, long robe of a variety of fabrics. It usually is worn over a short-sleeved white T-shirt.

appreciated in the Kuwaiti culture. Kuwaitis, it turns out, have strong religious and personal beliefs that discourage women from being exposed to the public eye in any way. Islamic teaching dictates that a man's clothing cover at least from his waist to his knees. The requirements are much more strict for women as the interpretation of the Islamic "dress code," obviously in stark contrast with prevailing styles in Europe and America, clearly demands that all parts of the woman's body, except the face,[28] hands and feet, be covered in public. They don't sell many bikinis at the Kuwaiti *souk*.

Unfortunately, we failed to invest any energy in learning about Kuwait's social code and customs. After all, we ignorantly assumed that whatever was acceptable in America was sure to be accepted in Kuwait. How naive Americans can be!

During the remainder of our first visit to Kuwait and on each subsequent stay, we have attempted to pay a great deal of attention to the various types and styles of clothing the "locals" prefer to wear. Almost without exception, men wear the traditional *dishdasha* as everyday business and casual wear. The primary difference between the business or formal *dishdasha* and the loose garment that is worn around the house is in the finish tailoring. The business *dishdasha* is typically a more tailored fit with cuffed sleeves, finished collar and breast pockets. Generally speaking, if you see an Arab man in Kuwait not wearing a *dishdasha*, he is most likely one of the thousands of the non-Kuwaiti Arabs living and working in Kuwait.

We have noticed that the *dishdasha* color and fabric selection varies with the seasons of the year.

---

[28] Many of the very conservative women, especially Bedouins, also cover their face to avoid tempting men to think evil thoughts.

During the extremely hot summers, white cotton blends dominate. However, as the weather changes and temperatures begin to fall, a wide variety of shades, mostly gray, blue and brown in wool blends, begin to appear. During the winter months, many Kuwaiti men also exchange their pure white *gatra* for a red and white checked head cloth (*shemagh*). This *shemagh* style headdress has become recognizable throughout the world due to the worldwide exposure received by the Palestine Liberation Organization's (PLO) leader, Yasar Arafat, wearing his black-and-white checked head covering. Just as it does in America, personal taste has a great deal to do with the way men dress in Kuwait. Often you will see a considerable amount of mixing and matching to reflect the individual's personal choices.

After you have been in Kuwait for some time, you begin to realize that the Kuwaitis are every bit as fashion conscious as Americans. The style options are more limited than those presented to the American consumer, but variations in color, fabric, and quality of workmanship become important. Fussy buyers would never purchase an "off-the-shelf" *dishdasha*. The discerning Kuwaiti clotheshorse has a favorite tailor who will carefully measure to assure the proper fit. On special occasions men will also wear a cloak or "*beshtt*" over their *dishdasha*. These cloaks are hand sewn and embroidered along the edges in gold thread imported from France or Germany. Made from the finest hand-woven camel-wool, a top quality *beshtt* can sell for hundreds of dollars.

On our third trip to Kuwait, Adnan took us to his tailor and had *dishdashas* custom made for Davin and me. Granted, we do not look exactly like Arabs, but we often wear these extremely comfortable garments when relaxing at home. Our *dishdashas* also make great conversation pieces when strangers, unaware of the Lambert family's Kuwaiti connection, come to visit.

In addition to wearing my *dishdasha*, another Kuwaiti habit I have embraced is the constant manipulating and twirling of a string of simple little beads. These beads - - I have seen some rare and very expensive strings among the Kuwaiti elite - - vary in size, bead shape, and material. However, with very few exceptions, whenever you see a Kuwaiti man in almost any casual or social setting, you will also see him giving his beads a workout, rolling them, spinning them around and around his fingers, or exchanging them from hand to hand. [29]

Many people think the beads are similar to the Catholic Rosary and serve a distinct purpose in prayer. Actually, I learned from a close Kuwaiti friend that these ever-present strings of beads are called "worry beads" and that most Kuwaiti men have simply developed a reliance on them to satisfy their need to keep their hands occupied. This same friend sheepishly explained, "My father used to tell me when I was a young, maturing boy, that if I didn't keep my hands busy playing with my worry beads, I might be tempted to play with something else."

At first glance, it appears that Kuwaiti women have an even more narrow range of options than do the men. In fact, in public the older, traditional Kuwaiti women will typically be clad from head to foot in a discreet black cloak (*abbaya*), while her face will be completely covered with a black veil (*bushiya*). However, rumor has it that what you see may not be what

---

[29] Originally, worry beads or "misbah" were used after or between prayers to count chanting words. The string may consist of 33, 66 or 99 beads. *Misbah* commonly seen in modern times are often the smaller variety and are used to occupy hands when they are free.

you get! Frequently, the *abbaya* shrewdly conceals garments of brilliant color and beautiful texture. Kuwaiti women enjoy wearing beautiful clothes, and they can afford to take advantage of the wide choice of the finest fabrics imported from throughout the world.

In recent trips to Kuwait we have noticed a significant increase in the number of women, especially young adults and women electing to enter the work force, thereby casting aside the traditional conservative black clothing in favor of more modern and colorful Middle Eastern styles, or even up-scale American and European fashions. No skin-tight jeans, shorts or miniskirts can be seen, but you can definitely sense the American influence as you stroll through the Kuwait University campus during class change times. We could just as easily have been mixing with students at UCLA, Stanford, The Ohio State University or The University of Michigan - - universities which, by the way, many of these Kuwaiti undergraduates' fathers attended before Kuwait University was established in 1966.

The Regency Palace Hotel,[30] which has served as our headquarters on each of our visits, frequently hosts Kuwaiti social gatherings, birthday celebrations, and parties associated with weddings and other special events. The environment and frivolity is very similar to the scene you see on Friday night in an American bar or an English pub - - with one exception, no alcohol! The gala activities and parties associated with a wedding are most elaborate and exciting to watch, especially in regard to Kuwaiti women. We have learned from friends that the Kuwaiti wedding party combines tradi-

---

[30] Iraqi troops set the Regency Palace ablaze as they withdrew from Kuwait. The damage was extensive, leaving only a blackened shell. Restaurants in the hotel reopened in mid-1992, but no schedule for hotel completion has been announced.

tional and modern activities. The bride and the groom have their own separate parties in a hotel or at a relative's house where they each greet members of the other's family, enjoy Kuwaiti music, dinner and dancing.

During one of these "girls night out" events, we commandeered one of the best Regency Palace lobby couches situated as close to the hotel entrance as possible. Hoping to avoid appearing rude or impolite, we attempted to be subtle, but maintaining a low profile was very difficult. It was a people-watcher's dream. A seemingly endless stream of Mercedes[31] pulled up to the hotel entry way, each unloading groups of women of all ages. They obviously had come to have fun. Everyone was smiling and laughing (unfortunately for us they were speaking Arabic), as the stories flew faster than a rumor in an American coffee break room.

None of the dull, basic black for these women. They came to show off their finest wardrobe. The event could easily have been a high society fashion show at the New York Palace Hotel, as women in gorgeous, multi-colored silk ensembles, each one more beautiful than the preceding, made their way toward the party room.

Those women who had chosen not to cover their faces revealed a natural Kuwaiti beauty highlighted with a wide variety of expertly applied makeup. Elaborate, but tasteful, necklaces, rings, and bracelets completed the festive look. Once they were inside the wedding party room, the doors were closed, and the rule was strictly "no men allowed." Only the colorful Arab

---

[31] Although the Mercedes Benz remains very popular in Kuwait, the "car of choice" for everyday family use in Kuwait seems to be the fullsize Chevrolet Caprice (white or navy blue). Tens of thousands have been imported since the end of the Iraqi occupation.

music and the frequent uproars of laughter coming from behind the doors confirmed that the women were having a wonderful time.

Young Kuwaiti children and teenagers provide perhaps the best example of the merging of the old and new in fashion trends. These small boys and girls are well-traveled, and it shows in the clothes they wear. Shirts advertising everything from the Hard Rock Cafe to Teenage Mutant Ninja Turtles can be seen in the shops and on the playgrounds after school. For more formal occasions the kids slip into their European wardrobes, recently purchased on one of their parent's frequent shopping trips to London or Paris. However, local tailors continue to make garments in all sizes and, much like in America, it is not unusual to see young boys and girls out for dinner or just walking along the sea front dressed just like mom or dad - - the girls in a "*hejab*" or scarf and the boys in their *dishdashas*.

The Kuwaiti clothing is not the only thing that catches the first-time visitor's attention. Kuwaitis, in my observations, do not hesitate to publicly demonstrate their feelings of compassion and friendship, especially among men. On my first trip to Kuwait, I was surprised to see adult men walking hand-in-hand as they talked, and I was very curious about the sight of men hugging and kissing each other on the cheek. I soon found out that these actions are common among long-time friends and close relatives, who have not seen each other in some time. Now that I better understand the culture, I consider it an honor when I return to Kuwait or host Kuwaiti friends in the United States, and I am greeted with kisses to alternating cheeks. Some say the number of kisses exchanged is an indicator of the closeness of the friendship between the two men (I have seen as many as six kisses exchanged), but I have been unable to confirm this claim.

As a result of our first Kuwaiti airport adventure, we committed ourselves to looking beyond the obvious outward personal appearance in search of the humanity which resides in all people. We are glad we took the time to peer beneath the surface, for what we found in the people of Kuwait was warmth, charm, compassion, humor, family devotion, respect for others and an undeniably strong sense of national pride. These are character traits worthy of admiration and emulation. We have also discovered that some Kuwaiti people can be impatient, self-serving, extremely demanding, and even rude at times. Our conclusion: the people of Kuwait are not so very different from American people. They have their strengths and weaknesses, good and bad days, just like Americans, and they dearly love their country, just as we do.

The best way to learn about Kuwaiti people is to spend time with them. Being somewhat socially inclined, we had no problem implementing this "mix with the natives" strategy. Almost from our first day in Kuwait, we looked for opportunities to become part of the daily Kuwaiti routine. We wanted to experience Kuwait from the inside, not as outsiders looking in. It was easier for some than others. For example, I am the most reserved one in the family, and, typically, I rely heavily on my wife, Carolyn, and my daughter, Erin, to initiate the conversations, especially in unfamiliar surroundings. Carolyn is so good at making new friends that it has been said she can learn a complete stranger's life story in the course of a short elevator ride.

Much to my dismay, this "let Carolyn and Erin do the talking" philosophy was almost totally ineffective in the segregated Kuwaiti social environment. Kuwaitis absolutely love to socialize. Primarily, however, men socialize with men, and women socialize strictly with women. Exceptions to this separation policy are seen during mealtimes when the company is frequently mixed, but even on those occasions, conversations will tend to gravitate to the universally common man-to-man or woman-to-woman.

Our friend, Adnan, knowing that we sincerely wanted to learn all we could about Kuwait, graciously invited Davin and me to join him and "the guys" at a neighborhood gathering. It was Sunday, and we had only been in Kuwait three days. Carolyn, my social safety net, was not invited. Adnan had barely extended the invitation when I could feel my palms become moist in anticipation of being thrown into this large group of Arabic-speaking strangers. My mind began searching for an acceptable reason for declining this unique opportunity to actually experience a piece of Kuwaiti culture. Too late! Carolyn thought it was a great idea and politely accepted for us.

That Sunday night Davin and I learned something about Kuwaiti men that continues to amaze us. Based upon our observations, the men in Kuwait actually enjoy socializing and talking MORE than the women. The core of the Kuwaiti male social structure seems to rest squarely on the concept of frequent group interaction. The formal name for these gab fests is "*diwaniya*," and they are conducted in the reception room or *diwan* of the host's home.

Over the years, Kuwaiti customs have gradually evolved so that the division of a house into distinctly separate men's and women's quarters, as was true in the past, is no longer typical. However, even the modern Kuwaiti house is designed in such a way that segregated social lives can be accommodated when required. Most houses have a central courtyard, and nearly all homes have a separate room or suit of rooms dedicated to the men's *diwaniya*. The average *diwan* is a spacious room with seating around the wall on three sides. The room we were in for our first *diwaniya* experience was very large (25'x50') and elaborately furnished.

Among the Kuwaitis, the question of who comes to the *diwaniya*, how many men regularly attend (40-50 men is not unusual) and how luxurious the amenities can be a significant social barometer. The higher the business or governmental rank of those men in attendance, as well as their numbers elevates the status of the *diwaniya*. (His Highness the Amir of Kuwait conducts and attends *diwaniyas* regularly in order to keep in touch with the needs and opinions of the Kuwaiti people) We were told that affluent families often appear to be competing to see which one can construct the biggest and best facility to house their family's *diwaniya*. These impressive *diwans* are oftentime separate from the main house and can be compared favorably to some of the finest luxury homes in America.

Just as we had learned with the clothing, however, it soon became obvious to us that it is not the size or external appearance of the *diwan*, or the number of men participating, that is most important. Rather, it is the process that takes place during the *diwaniya* itself that contributes to sustaining Kuwaiti social culture. The atmosphere is one of a male social club with family members, friends and neighbors all coming together to have refreshments, play cards, or even just watch television. Most likely, however, the topic of conversation will eventually center on business or politics.

These *diwaniyas*, which usually begin in the early evening, and sometimes do not conclude until well after midnight when the last person grows weary from talking, have been both informative and entertaining for us.

If the men are talking directly to us, they will speak in
English; however, the majority of the time everyone is
speaking at a very rapid pace in Arabic. Adnan, thankfully, attempted to interpret for us whenever he could,
but at any one time, up to a dozen men might be speaking simultaneously. Surprisingly, everyone seemed to
understand what was being said. I have witnessed this
difficult feat occasionally among members of our
American neighborhood gourmet dinner group, but
I never thought I would see men who had become so skilled in this type of simultaneous group
communication.

Occasionally, the exchanges became rather
heated and demonstrative, and the attendees at the
diwaniya quickly took sides and graphically expounded
upon the particular subject being addressed. The general topic of politics, particularly the Kuwaiti National
Assembly process, always seemed to generate the highest level of involvement and enthusiasm. Regardless of
the differences of opinions, however, and how heated
the debate became, once the discussion terminated,
whether or not a consensus was reached, the Kuwaiti
men appeared to forget their differences and parted as
friends, already looking forward to the next *diwaniya*.

Because the tradition of the *diwaniya* is an integral part of Kuwaiti social life, on any given night
hundreds of sessions are taking place in every Kuwaiti
city or suburb. Kuwaiti men do not - - although they
easily could - - spend every evening at a *diwaniya*. In a
typical family, for example, the father will host his
family and friends on Saturday or Sunday, while his son
will entertain on Thursday or Friday. Some of the Kuwaiti men we have come to know intentionally limit
their attendance to only one or two *diwaniyas* each
week.

Although they employ a slightly different approach, the women of Kuwait are not exactly social recluses, although you will generally find women at home once their husbands have returned from working or visiting. Even the older, more conservative women in Kuwait, who are reluctant to leave their home at any time for the sake of socializing, have discovered that the telephone provides a convenient and timely means of combining their traditional personal privacy with active sociability.

The Kuwaiti woman of the 1990s has refined the use of the telephone to a degree that would challenge any American teenager. This mastery of the telephone system has led to the creation of a sophisticated and well used communication network, linking friends and relatives. When you add to this electronic "grape vine," and the freedom and mobility provided by the automobile, it becomes clear that any traditional obstacles facing a Kuwaiti woman who desires to establish and maintain an active and productive social calendar have been eliminated. In this regard, Kuwaiti women may actually be in a better position than their counterparts in America, since the majority of Kuwaiti women, housewives and working women alike, have the distinct advantage of live-in household help, which means that more free time can be used for the social process.

We feel that we have at least begun to understand the people of Kuwait through attending social events, working with them in a professional environment, visiting their schools, participating in *diwaniyas*, and simply going out into the public setting and watching people operate within their own environment. We have been fortunate to have had these frequent opportunities to visit Kuwait. But perhaps the representative example of what, in our opinion, is at the core of our sincere regard and respect for the people of Kuwait is an event which took place on an August day in 1987, not in Kuwait, but at the Seattle Sheraton Hotel and Towers.

The eye-opening incident involved a small child and several well-dressed Kuwaiti businessmen. The men were clustered around a large hotel lobby table deeply involved in serious discussions about their next multi-million dollar investment scheme. The young child, a girl probably not more than three years old, had become separated from her parents and inadvertently wandered into the middle of the intensely focused Kuwaiti business meeting.

Everything stopped. The Kuwaiti men set their papers down and looked at the tiny intruder. But, instead of reflecting irritation, the eyes of the Kuwaiti men glowed with concern and friendship. Each man went out of his way to make the lost child feel secure and welcome. Nothing else seemed to be important at the time. The business deals were temporarily forgotten. These tough, articulate executives were almost magically transformed into surrogate fathers for this little lost child. To a man, they became swept up in the game of seeing who could elicit the biggest smile. As observers, it was obvious to us that the display of concern and caring for this child was sincere. Their interest in making the youngster feel comfortable and at ease was genuine. None of the men resented the lost work time. Once the little girl was reunited with her relieved parents, the men, as quickly as they had become substitute fathers, resumed their roles as hard-driving businessmen.

The health, welfare, and happiness of family, friends and strangers alike are very important matters for Kuwaitis. Kuwaiti family ties are something to be envied and emulated in these time of single parents and geographically separated relatives. Kuwaitis are famous for their worldwide business and pleasure trips, but I know from personal involvement with these traveling executives that they cannot return to Kuwait and their families quickly enough.

The compassionate Kuwaiti's reach extends far beyond blood relatives and close friends.[32] More than once I have seen a Kuwaiti, without solicitation, inconspicuously slip money into the hand of a total stranger, obviously in need, who passed them on the sidewalk.[33] I have seen it happen in Kuwait, and I have seen it happen on the streets of Seattle and San Francisco. Few people notice the spontaneous generosity, and the anonymous Kuwaiti benefactor does not expect or desire any recognition or thanks.

As a rule, the Kuwaiti people seem fairly relaxed and able to deal productively with whatever stress is introduced into their usually smooth-running lives. But, beware the Kuwaiti who feels that his family or close friends have been seriously threatened or that his business trust and confidence have been intentionally violated. A Kuwaiti who has been wronged in these ways will be very unforgiving and will, almost without exception, expect some form of reparation or consideration.

The closeness and devotion within the Kuwaiti family is as important today as it ever was in times past. However, the structure and composition of the family has changed dramatically over the past several decades. In the first two hundred years of Kuwait's existence, families often included a husband with multiple

---

[32] Kuwait, as a country, has always been very charitable. Since 1961 Kuwait has granted over 300 loans totalling $5 billion toward assistance to other Arab states and Third World developing countries.

[33] Islam attaches no shame to begging and much virtue to charity.

wives (four wives are allowed under Islamic Law) and ten or more children. Although multiple wives remain acceptable under Islamic law, during our visits to Kuwait we have failed to meet anyone in our generation (born after 1940) who has taken advantage of this opportunity. In fact, when we quizzed our married male Kuwaiti friends, some of whom returned to Kuwait from their educational stay in the U.S. with American wives, concerning the multiple-wife option, the response has been generally something like, "you must be joking. I can't afford the one I have." The attitude of the modern Kuwaiti man seems to be consistent with something Abigail Van Buren once said, "In Biblical times, a man could have as many wives as he could afford. Just like today."[34]

As times have changed and the monogamous relationships have become normal, dramatic changes have occurred in the approach to finding a mate in Kuwaiti society. Young men now meet their wives in Kuwait, in other Arab countries, and, in many cases, in foreign countries as they travel or attend school (1986 Kuwaiti statistics indicated almost 1,000 Kuwaiti men are married to non-Kuwaiti women.) However, there are still many of the matches and eventual marriages arranged in the traditional Kuwaiti manner.

Once a Kuwaiti man has reached the age range of 25-29, it is likely he will make a request for his mother to begin the marriage process by visiting the prospective bride's family to ask for their daughter's hand in marriage to her son. Unlike the American method where tradition indicates the father plays a much bigger role, in Kuwait the mothers assume most of the respon-

---

[34] Regarding multiple wives, The Koran clearly states in its Chapter on Women in Verse 2: "Marry whom you like of women, two, three and four, but if you are afraid to be unjust, only one."

sibility in implementing the marriage process. During her visit the boy's mother and the girl's family exchange information such as age (the average age for Kuwaiti women to marry is between 20-24), occupation, and amount of education. In past Kuwaiti generations, some of these questions were not necessary to ask, since it was not unusual to find marriages among relatively close family members. For example, it was common to find first cousins as husband and wife. In fact, in the older generation of still-living Kuwaitis, these first-cousin marriages have endured exceptionally well. However, today's generation of Kuwaitis frequently marry outside the family; or, if they do select a spouse from within the larger family, it will be a distant third or fourth cousin.

We have been told, however, that the issue of religious compatibility remains an important one to many Kuwaitis when considering a marriage partner. For example, many marriages in Kuwait match partners from either the Shiite or Sunni Sect of Islam.[35] Although not encouraged, Islam does not forbid inter-religion or inter-nationality marriages. The only exception is that a Muslim cannot marry someone who does not believe in the concept of the existence of one God.

If the young man's mother and the young woman's family agree that the marriage idea is good, the two potential mates must agree to proceed to the next step - - a meeting between the two is arranged at the prospective bride's house. Other women must be present when they meet, but no men are allowed. In a

---

[35] The fundamental difference between Shiite and Sunni sects is Shiite believe that Iman Ali was appointed by Prophet Mohammad to be his successor. Sunnis believe that the position was vacant after the Profit Muhammad's death and should be occupied by someone appointed by the elite. Sunnis hold a solid majority among the Kuwaiti population.

very conservative Muslim household, the prospective groom does not see the woman's face prior to this meeting and will not see it during their first meeting. The couple spends about half-an-hour talking and asking each other questions during this initial session.

Once this meeting has concluded, the young woman tells her mother if she is interested in the young man, and the young man also tells his mother if he is interested in continuing the process. If either party lacks interest, the process ends and the potential marriage is no more. But, if the couples like one another, then the fathers, brothers, and uncles become involved and meet to discuss the formal, more business-like portions of the marriage arrangements.

One of the first items of discussion is the "*mahr*", or bride's payment. It is traditional in the Kuwaiti culture for the prospective husband to provide his wife-to-be with the *mahr* prior to the marriage (in most other cultures it is the bride's family who must present the dowry to the husband-to-be, which is the same concept as the *mahr*). Often times, the young woman will receive beautiful jewelry in addition to any payment of money. This *mahr* represents the prospective groom's serious intentions about the marriage and allows the girl to prepare adequately for the wedding.

I was in the gold *souk* one day with Carolyn, Erin, and Marnie when a soon-to-be husband was selecting some jewelry for his *mahr*. We all stared in amazement as the merchant took each of the man's selections and added them to the stack being weighed (gold in Kuwait is considered legal tender and is bought and sold based on the precise weight). When the merchant finally added the last piece, he informed the proud purchaser that his total cost was KD5,500 ($18,700). The man just smiled broadly as he paid the merchant in cash, obviously imagining how pleased his betrothed was going to be with his purchase. When we told our Kuwaiti friends about the big purchase we had seen, they shared with us that the price of wedding jewelry often reaches as much as $50,000.

Once the *mahr* has been received, the future bride begins to buy her trousseau and starts planning her wedding parties. At this point in the marriage process, the man and woman can talk freely with each other - - but only on the telephone!

The actual religious binding of the couple is called "*melcha*" and is marked by a big party for the relatives of both families. At this time, the marriage contract is formally issued, and the couple is legally married. However, the next phase is really more like an American engagement, since the couple does not live together, but is allowed to go out alone together on dates.

Sometime later, and the amount of time can vary from a few months to a year, two huge wedding parties are held - - one for the woman and her family, and a separate one for the man and his family. When these parties are over, the couple becomes man and wife in the American sense and begins living together.

Getting married in Kuwait can be a rewarding experience in more ways than one. The Kuwaiti government grants a "marriage loan" to those male citizens marrying for the first time. The sum is KD4,000 ($13,000), half of which does not have to be repaid while the other half is treated as a normal loan but is repaid without interest.

When the couple begins a family, more rewards than the simple joys of having a baby are in store. The Kuwaiti government pays the family KD50 ($170) each month for every child. There is no limit on the number of children, and the government payment continues until the child marries or begins to work, regardless of age.

What happens if sometime later either the husband or wife decides they have made the wrong choice of spouse? Well, some would tell you that divorce in Kuwait is as easy as the man saying, "I divorce you," three times to his wife, and the marriage is officially over. The Kuwaitis, like everyone else around the world, sometimes wish it were that easy. Fortunately, the legal system has a major role to play in modern-day Kuwait in order to insure fair and equitable treatment of both parties undertaking the serious matter of a divorce. The laws are complex and very similar to those that exist in America, with each case examined individually based on its unique circumstances. The custody of the children must be decided as well as how much alimony will be paid and how much money will be provided for child support. The divorce process can be rather lengthy, depending on the circumstances.

The most recently available divorce statistics for Kuwait (1986) indicate that about 10 out of every 1,000 (one percent) Kuwaiti marriages end in divorce. This figure represents Kuwaiti citizens only. Adding in the non-Kuwaiti figures the number drops substantially to a composite average of only about four divorces in 1,000 marriages.

After examining the marriage and divorce processes and after considering the difficult economic conditions around the world, you can begin to understand why most Kuwaiti men feel that taking on more than one wife in today's society would be an incredibly difficult challenge.

As the number of wives has decreased, partially due to economics, so has the number of children. Despite strong encouragement from the Kuwait govern-ment for early marriages and larger Kuwaiti families, most of the couples we encountered had between three and five children.

In talking with fathers in these modern Kuwaiti families, I learned that economic factors were actually only a small part of the rationale behind having fewer children. Instead, the need for more intense and person-alized attention to their children's education, combined with the Kuwaiti parents' unrelenting devotion to en-suring their offsprings' personal and financial success, resulted in the realization that there is a limited amount of time available to accomplish these critical parental duties. The more children, the less time for each. Obvi-ous conclusion: fewer children. In wealthy circles, there is another option: have larger families but hire more household help to handle some of the parenting chores. Some families have experimented with this approach, but Kuwaiti parents have been concerned when their children naturally begin to emulate the characteristics, expressions, and even cultural philosophies of the for-eign workers, often in direct conflict with accepted Kuwaiti practices and beliefs.

Currently most Kuwaiti families are attempting to achieve a delicate balance or blend, in which the hired workers accomplish primarily task-oriented household duties, errands, watching very small chil-dren, and preliminary food preparation before the Ku-waiti mother actually cooks the meal, utilizing pre-ferred Kuwaiti spices and traditional cooking methods.

Kuwait has often been criticized by America and Europe for its openly lavish and pampered lifestyle. Much of this criticism has been aimed at the extensive use of immigrant labor, especially in regard to the comparatively simple, but important, tasks of child-rearing, cleaning house, and cooking. I must admit that my first impression was consistent with that of my fellow Americans. It seemed that some Kuwaitis were lazy, uninvolved parents who took advantage of the immigrants to whom they freely delegated responsibility for raising their children and completing all basic chores.

Further investigation, however, proved once again that our first impressions were grossly inaccurate. The household workers, primarily from India, Sri Lanka, Indonesia, Pakistan, and the Philippines, receive paid transportation to and from Kuwait and are paid a salary of approximately KD45 ($150) a month. They also receive a small sleeping room, free board, a generous clothing allowance, and two months of paid vacation at the end of their two-year contracts. Although the salary may seem small by American standards, the household help we met considered working in Kuwait a real economic opportunity, as $150 a month is often ten times what the same immigrants would be earning for a month of hard labor in their home countries.

The household workers, who appear very content and well treated by their Kuwaiti employers, send most of their money home to help support their starving, destitute relatives. Some Kuwaitis have kept the same help for so many years that they have almost become part of the family.

I will always remember our first visit to a Kuwaiti Minister's beautiful home. We had been sitting in the large living room talking with the Minister and his wife when suddenly we looked up and saw a small parade of women dressed in sparkling clean and crisply ironed white uniforms marching toward us. Each carried a silver tray filled with cakes, cookies, and tea. The servers were members of the Minister's household staff, and it was obvious to us that they were experts in the role.

The Minister's wife told us later that these women, as well as the family driver, had been with her family for many years. After the Iraqi invasion, we saw her in London waiting to take her children back to liberated Kuwait. She told us that she felt so strongly about the welfare of her household help and driver that she had continued to pay them their full salaries, even though they had been forced to flee Kuwait and return to their native countries. The Minister's wife has pledged to do everything she can to arrange for all of them to eventually return to Kuwait, if they wish to do so.

If the Kuwaiti people are guilty of anything in regard to using immigrant labor, it may simply be overindulgence. Often, very wealthy Kuwaiti families employ four or five household workers in addition to drivers and gardeners. In reality, the use of hired help to perform less than desirable tasks (as we say, "I have better things to do with my time") is not exactly a foreign concept to Americans. Even in middle-class American families, it is not unusual to hire someone to mow the lawn, iron the cotton shirts, or baby-sit the children. The two big differences are: first, in America only the wealthy can afford permanent live-in house-keepers, gardeners, and cooks; second, those workers who are hired are usually U.S. citizens.

Thanks to the wealth from oil, coupled with shrewd business dealings and wise benevolent government policies, almost every Kuwaiti family is wealthy enough to take advantage of the availability of inexpensive, qualified and eager immigrant labor. (See Chapters 11 and 12 for more about immigrant labor.)

5

UNDERSTANDING ISLAM

The Way of Life in Kuwait

Erin Lambert

"Religion is a candle inside a multicolored lantern. Everyone looks through a particular color, but the candle is always there."

Mohammed Negulb

In 609 A.D., during the month of Ramadan, Muhammad Ibn Abdallah Ibn Abd Al-Muttalib Ibn Hashim sat meditating in the cave of Hira, near Mecca. On this one special night it is said Muhammad, the future prophet, had a vision.[36]

A voice said to him: "I am Gabriel, the angel sent by God to announce to you that you have been appointed by God[37] to communicate His messages, His revelations to humanity." And the first revelation Muhammad received was this:

Recite in the name of your Lord, The Creator
Who created man from a clot of blood,
Recite! Your Lord is the most bounteous One
Who by this pen has taught,
Taught man things he did not know.

---

[36] Muslims believe Muhammad was the last of the Prophets. Jesus Christ and the Old Testament Prophets were his predecessors.

[37] Allah is the Arabic translation of God. Christians, Jews, and Muslims all believe in and worship the same God. Arab Christians refer to God as Allah. However, most Arabs prefer using God not Allah in English language writing.

These famous words form the first five verses of the 96th chapter of the Holy Koran,[3] the holy book by which all Muslims, one fifth of the world's population, live. The remainder of the Koran contains all the revelations made to Muhammad by God through the archangel, Gabriel, during the great prophet's last twenty years of life.

The Holy Koran teaches Muslims the lessons of God's absolute power and unity as well as recognition as the ultimate creator of the universe. It also teaches that God is just and merciful and wishes man to repent and purify himself while on earth so that he can attain Paradise (Heaven) after death. Muslims support the idea that God sends prophets with sacred books to teach man his duty to God and to his fellow human beings. The Holy Koran forms the religious foundation and establishes the fundamental principals for the Islamic faith. The Muslims believe that the Koran is an earthly book bound between two covers and is a copy of the "Well Preserved Tablet," an eternal book that is preserved in Heaven.[39] The principals established by the Koran forbid the representation of human and animal figures in the form of statues or monuments, denounce lending money at a high or unlawful rate of interest (usury), disallow participation in games of chance

---

[38] The Arabic-to-English spelling of the Islamic Religion's most sacred book most frequently seen in Europe and the Middle East is: The Holy Qur'an. However, for this book the spelling used is that which is most commonly seen in American publications and reference material: The Holy Koran or Koran.

[39] The recording of the Holy Koran appears to have been accomplished in separate volumes before being consolidated into one. Chapters are not arranged in any topical or chronological order. The only order that is apparent is that the longest chapter (286 verses) comes first and the shortest chapter (three verses) is last.

(gambling), and, like the Bible, forbid lying, stealing, adultery, and murder. In early times the punishment for transgression was based upon the Old Testament concept of retaliation - - "an eye for an eye and a tooth for a tooth."

In addition to these basic principals, the Koran also teaches Muslims to honor their parents, show kindness to workers, protect the orphaned and the widowed, and extend charity to the poor. At the same time, Islam's Holy Book speaks of the virtues of faith in God, patience, kindness, honesty, industry, courage, and generosity, while condemning mistrust, impatience, and cruelty.

Basically, Islam teaches that life on earth is a period of testing and preparation for the life to come. As the angels in heaven are thought to record good and bad deeds, a person should try his best to be good and help others. One must also trust in God's justice and mercy. Death is not feared by Muslims , for it is the gateway to eternal life, which is pictured by Muslims as a garden with flowing streams, luscious flowers, fruits, and richly covered couches.

In order to understand the effect Islam has on the everyday lives of the Kuwaiti people, it is necessary to understand the central importance of the religion in Arabic culture and the fundamental teachings of Muhammad.[40] To help achieve this understanding, allow me to draw a mental picture of the holy city of Mecca, during the seventh century A.D.

With a population of 10,000, Mecca was a prosperous trading center, through which passed caravans

---

[40] *Sunna* meaning "the trodden path" is the word used generally to represent the practices based on the deeds and sayings of the Prophet Muhammed.

of silk, spices, and perfumes from around the world. Mecca was a well organized "city-state" with a council of ten hereditary oligarchies. At the time, the government was comprised of a series of ministries - - justice , defense, worship, citizen consultations, external relations, and other civic affairs. The leadership positions were held by a mostly generous, honest group who were always anxious and willing to help feed the poor during times of famine. The local people had even set up an "order of chivalry" which had a main objective of protecting the interests of foreigners who had been unjustly treated while in Mecca.

Mecca was most celebrated at the time for a temple known as the Ka'ba, a cubical building said to have been built by Adam and later restored by Abraham. Around the outside of the temple were the figures of 360 idols who looked out from the walls of the vast building overlooking the city. Inside the temple, among the figures portrayed on the frescoes, were the Virgin Mary and the infant Jesus. The black stone in one corner marked the place where the ritual procession around the temple began. The annual pilgrimage to Mecca brought Arab people from all over the peninsula to pledge their devotion to God before this same black stone, in the corner of the Ka'ba.

It was here, in Mecca, that Muhammad was born to a merchant family in about 570 A.D. Even in his early years, Muhammad displayed exceptional qualities. In particular, he earned the name of Al-Amin (worthy of confidence), for his integrity in business. Historians have often tried to shed light on Muhammad's character. It is said that Muhammad once had a young slave named Zaid Ibn Harithah, who had been captured during a war. Eventually, after searching for years, the boy's father, a chief of a big tribe, found the boy and offered Muhammad a large ransom in exchange for his son. Muhammad declared that he would free the boy for nothing if he willingly agreed to go with his father. After deep thought, Zaid announced that he preferred to stay with Muhammad. Muhammad was deeply moved by this action and immediately set the boy free and took him to the Ka'ba and declared that he was going to adopt his former slave as his son.

It was also here, in Mecca that Muhammad later became discontented with everyday life and began to spend a great deal of time in meditation, in the cave of Hira. For five years, Muhammad went into seclusion during the entire month of Ramadan, and it was during the fifth year in meditation that he had his first vision of the Archangel Gabriel and thus began the preaching to the people of Mecca. It is the belief in Muhammad's preachings that continues to motivate and guide Muslims throughout the world.

A Muslim is a person who believes in all messengers and prophets sent by God throughout history, including the final prophet Muhammad, who Muslims believe succeeded Jesus Christ and the Old Testament prophets. They believe that Jesus was a prophet of God, as was Muhammad; however, Muslims do not believe that Jesus was the Son of God. The followers of Islam accept the revelations and teachings of Muhammad as written in the Holy Koran as the last divine scripture and believe that these revelations and teachings are to be the guiding aspect in the life of all Muslims.

The foundation of Islam resides among the 114 chapters which comprise the Holy Koran. The contents of these chapters are considered the "code of ethics" for Muslims - - known throughout the world as the "Five Pillars of Islam." These Five Pillars are acceptance of the confession of faith ("There is no God if not God and

Muhammad is the Messenger of God."); saying daily prayers (*Salat*); paying taxes (*Zakat*),[41] which is similar to the tithe mentioned in the Bible; making a pilgrimage to Mecca (*Hajj*); and fasting during the ninth month of the Muslim year,[42] Ramadan.

Upon our first visit to Kuwait, throughout the day we periodically heard what seemed like a half-chanting, half singing Arabic voice looming and echoing throughout the city. Whether we were relaxing in our hotel, shopping, eating or just visiting with friends, the penetrating voice of this unseen man would suddenly emerge from the sky. The strangest part was that, although our family heard the sound and repeatedly tried to determine its origin, as we looked around, no one else seemed to notice, or care, about this mysterious voice. Were we going mad? Were we the only ones hearing an Arabic man singing and chanting? We couldn't be sure, but we certainly hoped not.

It was a great relief when we finally learned that the voice was a holy man calling the Muslims in the city to prayer. Five times a day the Crier, or *Muezzin*, announces prayer time from the mosque tower. Prayer is an important part of a Muslim's life. *Fajr* is the prayer that begins roughly forty-five minutes before sunrise and lasts until the sun comes up. The *Zuhr* prayer begins

---

[41] *Zakat* and *Khums* are contributions in the amount of approximately twenty percent on their income, land and other valuables such as gold, silver, etc. The money is paid to Bait Al-Zakat (tax house) to be used in supporting a wide range of Islamic activities in Kuwait and abroad.

[42] The Muslim calendar starts with the date of the Prophet Muhammad's emigration from Mecca to Medina. This event took place on a Friday, July 16, A.D. 622. The Muslim calendar consists of 354 days distributed over twelve months. Like Leap Year in the 365 day Gregorian or Christian calendar, which starts with the birth of Jesus Christ, the Muslim calendar adds one day to the last month eleven times in every thirty years - or one extra day every 2.7 years.

when the sun is at its highest point and has just begun its journey back down the arc - - approximately noon. The prayer known as *'Asr* begins when the position of the sun forms a body's shadow that is equal to approximately two body lengths (approximately 3 p.m.). The fourth prayer in the Muslim's day is the *Maghrib,* and it is said after the sun has completely set and there is no more light reflecting off the clouds. *'Isha,* the final prayer of the day, begins about one and a half hours after the setting of the sun.

The Muslims take these prayers very seriously. There have been many occasions during our visits to Kuwait when our friends have excused themselves from a social setting in order to pray. In Kuwait, or even in the United States, when Kuwaiti business executives are attending a seminar, the daily schedule must always allow for breaks at the appropriate time of the day to enable those who wish to pray the opportunity to do so. Kuwait's local Safeway Store, one of the largest stores of its kind in the world, has constructed a mini-mosque on the second floor to ensure those shopping there will be able to pray anytime during the day.

I will never forget the time when we were stopped at a gas station filling the car's tank. About half way through the process, we heard the *Muezzin* calling Muslims to prayer. Immediately we noticed an old man unroll a small rug and neatly spread it on the gas station pavement. He fell to his knees and appeared totally unaware of anything else around him as he carried out his ritual worship to God.

On Friday, which for the Muslims is similar to the Jewish Sabbath and the Christian Sunday, Muslims are expected to attend noon prayers at a mosque. At the mosque the Muslim ceremonially washes his face, hands, and feet immediately before prayer to assure a state of cleanliness before

God. The *Iman*[43] faces Mecca. The men stand in rows
behind the Iman and the women stand behind the
men.[44] The prayers consist of reciting passages from the
Koran and repeating other phrases of praise to God.
Portions of this prayer process include bowing from the
hips and kneeling with the face to the ground. Typically, the Friday noon prayer is preceded by a sermon.

We are impressed with the fact that whether it
was in the privacy of their own homes, at social functions, in public buildings, or even at a local gas station,
the majority of Muslims in Kuwait are committed to
their faith and are never afraid or embarrassed to show
their devotion to God.

Although many prayers are said at home or, if
necessary, in a more public setting, as mentioned earlier, sometimes it is important for Muslims to go to
mosques to express some of their prayers.[45] In Kuwait
there are plenty of mosques to choose from - - try
approximately 630. Of these 630 mosques, which are
conveniently located in nearly every neighborhood,
close to sixty percent were built or paid for by individuals within a specific family and often times carry the
name of that family. The remainder of the mosques have
been built with government funds. Each local mosque
holds an average of 900 worshippers at one time. The

---

[43] The *Iman*, or prayer leader, is the chief officer of the mosque. The *Iman's*
main duty is to lead the people in prayer. Islam does not have an organized
priesthood or cleric hierarchy. The Symbol of Islam is a crescent and star,
which can be seen atop the mosques.
[44] Muslim women have the same basic requirements for prayer as men.
Women must cover themselves from head to toe, except face and hands.
Thee women are exempted from prayers during menstruation. While
women can go to the mosques for prayer, they pray in a separate room
isolated from the men.
[45] Christians and Jews can visit mosques on the condition that they are
clean (pure) with dry feet. Those who do not believe in a single God are not
permitted to enter the mosque.

obvious exception to this capacity is the Grand State Mosque, which is one of the most beautiful and most modern mosques in the Islamic world. The Grand State Mosque is located near the center of old Kuwait City and has been designed to accommodate up to 5,000 Muslims. It is quite a sight to stand in the busy streets of Kuwait City or in an isolated suburb when the *Muezzin* calls for prayer and watch as dozens of people suddenly begin making their way, some running, some walking, toward the mosque for their daily prayers.

The Islamic religion is one of great feasts and festivities. The best known of these is the month of Ramadan, when each and every Muslim fasts every day from dawn to dusk. We learned not to worry about the people suffering too long from hunger - - there is enough food consumed "after dusk" to satisfy even the biggest appetite. Many of these foods are special delicacies that only are prepared during the month of Ramadan.

As the end of the Ramadan period approaches and Kuwaitis prepare for the three-day Festival of the Breaking of the Fast, the Kuwait *souks* (markets) are very busy selling sweets, sugar, nuts, tea, incense, coffee, and sodas to be served to the many visitors on Eid al-Fitir,[46] which marks the official end of the Ramadan fast.

A significant part of the Eid al-Fitir is visiting. Although the visit to friends and relatives is short, each is, nevertheless, very important to Muslims. For a Muslim to not visit a friend or relative during this time, is the same as saying that the person is not important; therefore, everyone visits everyone!

At each visit, the hosts and guests exchange

---

[46] *Eid* is the Arabic word for holiday.

greetings, and visitors give the hosts' children money to spend at the local *souks*. Once the greetings and presents are exchanged, guests are served fruit juice, tea, nuts, and assorted sweets. The time spent visiting and eating is brief and, after refreshments are gone, incense is burned and good-byes are said as the guests move on to their next visit. This period of post-Ramadan visiting often goes on for 12 hours a day for several days.

Ramadan is not only a time for Kuwaitis to party late into the night. It is also a time for them to help those less fortunate. During the month, many families gather old clothing and household goods to be given to the needy. One of our good friends in Kuwait has a non-Kuwaiti family who comes to his home each year during Ramadan asking for food, money or clothing. Each year there is always a box of clothing and food ready and waiting, and our Kuwaiti friend usually provides some money to help this poor family with special needs they may have.

Another important Islamic holiday is Eid al-Adha, a four day *Eid* similar to that of Eid al-Fitir, which marks the willingness of Abraham to sacrifice his son and is the occasion of the annual pilgrimage to Mecca. This is actually considered the Great Festival by the Muslims, while the Breaking of the Fast is the Lesser Festival. The pilgrimage is concluded with the Festival of Sacrifice, when the Muslims symbolically sacrifice a sheep, goat, or camel and usually give the meat to the poor.

The Prophet Muhammad's birthday, the Ascension Day, which marks the ascension to heaven of the prophet Muhammad, and the Islamic New Year are all one day holidays that are observed by the Muslims. Among the Shiite sect of Islam, the death of Husain, a grandson of Muhammad, and the birth of Fatima,

Muhammad's daughter, are also often celebrated. The event in which Muslims perhaps take most pride and celebrate with parties and gifts, occurs when their child has memorized all 114 chapters, or *suras*, of the Holy Koran.[47]

Islam is not just a part of Kuwaitis' lives - - it is the way of life in Kuwait. Every detail of their lives revolves around Islam - from what they can and cannot eat, to what kind of pet is allowed. In the Islamic teaching the dog is considered an "unclean" animal and is not an option for a pet. Muslims, in fact are not to touch dogs. In fact, if they do happen to come in contact with a dog, they must carefully bathe themselves before saying their next prayers. Cleanliness is very important in Islam, and one must be "clean" before coming to God to pray.

One summer, while my father was conducting a Kuwaiti seminar in San Francisco, we were walking down the streets of the city with about thirty Kuwaiti Businessmen. We were on our way to the Pacific Coast Stock Exchange to learn how stocks were bought and sold. It had been an uneventful walk from the Hyatt on Union Square and we were almost to the Stock Exchange when a man - - and his big dog - - came walking toward our group. I have never seen a group of grown men move as fast as they did that day. The group divided down the middle, clearing a very large path, to allow the man - - and his dog - - to walk past untouched. At the time, I thought it strange that so many men could have been afraid of one dog. It was really an amusing sight to see. It was much later when I learned the Islamic reason behind their actions.

---

[47] Often times Islamic educational institutions require students to memorize all 77,934 words of the Holy Koran before being accepted.

Islam also plays a large role in deciding who is allowed to visit inside a Kuwaiti's home. One afternoon, while in Kuwait, my mother and I had spent the day talking and enjoying tea with some friends inside their beautiful home. There were no men in the room at the time, and all women, married and unmarried, had removed the sheer covers from their faces. All was well until my brother, who was nineteen years old at the time, attempted to come into the room. He was stopped and sternly reminded that there was a young lady of "marrying age" in the room who was not properly covered and that he would have to "keep out." This incident took place on our first trip to Kuwait, and Davin was confused and somewhat offended at the time. Later that day we explained to him that in a conservative Islamic household an unmarried girl is never to be seen with her hair uncovered by any man who is not related to her. Davin felt much better when he realized the rebuff wasn't because of anything personal against him.

While doing Kuwaiti seminars in San Francisco and Seattle, it seemed as if each day something would happen that would remind us of the subtle differences between the seminar participants from Kuwait and the American businessmen. For instance, upon our arrival in the seminar host city several days before the class was scheduled to begin, my dad and I met in the Kuwait Foundation for the Advancement of Sciences (KFAS) seminar director's room to go over last minute logistical details. Each year one of those details was an assignment to obtain information that would allow all participants to determine the exact time the sun would rise and set each day for the duration of the two-week seminar. We also had to identify the direction the participant would need to face to be looking toward Mecca. This information was all documented and provided as part of the participant's welcoming packet of information. Using this critical information about the sun's cycle and the direction of Mecca, the participant would be able to correctly fulfill his obligation for prayer.

Working with the Kuwaiti executives in the United States, Canada, Kuwait, or anywhere in the world, presents a challenge for hotels and restaurants in the area of food selection and preparation. The Islamic religion dictates some special needs which must be considered. Any pork products and all alcohol are strictly forbidden, and meat of any kind must be from animals that have been slaughtered and prepared according to Islamic standards.[48]

The requirement for complete absence of pork or anything that has even the smallest portion of pork content from a Kuwaiti's diet is absolute. For instance, when we are in Kuwait, we can still order pepperoni pizzas from Pizza Hut, but it is not pork pepperoni - - it is beef pepperoni from beef slaughtered and prepared in a Kuwait facility. Although the "fake" pork tastes very similar to the real thing, it is hard to get accustomed to having bacon and eggs or a ham and cheese sandwich - - without the bacon or the ham.

It is easy for the Kuwaitis to adhere to the strict standards in an Arab dominated environment, however, sometimes when the Kuwaitis are traveling the differences in language and the lack of their host's understanding of the Islamic requirements can present a serious problem. During a 1988 seminar in Seattle, I was sitting in the Sheraton Towers' lobby one evening with some Kuwaiti participants when they decided to

---

[48] These standards include: the animal must be killed quickly without pain using sharp instruments. All traces of blood must be removed by draining, washing, soaking and salting. Meat from animals that have been killed by hunters is not to be eaten.

have a late night snack. One of the men ordered a bacon burger, but politely ask the waitress to please hold the bacon. Well, of course, when the burger came it still had bacon on it. My Kuwaiti friend called the waitress back to the table and requested she ask the cook to make him another burger - - this time without the bacon. The waitress, clearly oblivious to the culturally-based rea-son for the simple request, responded with a smart-alec look, as she leaned over and simply removed the bacon from the burger, setting it on the side of his plate while she reminded her foreign guest how easy it was to fix his little problem. Unfortunately, the Kuwaiti had to be persistent in his request for a new hamburger, since the juices from the bacon had already soaked into the beef patty. When he finally was able to get his meal prepared correctly, he said to me, "She just doesn't understand." He was noticeably upset by the experience. On one hand, he did not want the waitress to draw the conclu-sion that he was just trying to be difficult, while on the other hand he wished that she would have attempted to understand the reason behind his unusual request so that the entire scene could have been avoided.

The actual method of food preparation used out-side Kuwait can present another serious problem. In Kuwait, since having or consuming alcohol is illegal, the people of Kuwait do not have to worry about the method of preparation used for the many Kuwaiti meal selections. However, outside of Kuwait it is often very hard for Kuwaitis to find restaurants that prepare food, especially the evening meals, without using some form of alcohol in the cooking process. Some argue that the alcohol used in food preparation is not a problem, since it is literally cooked off or evaporated in the process. However, strict Muslims will not eat anything prepared with alcohol. In fact, the strict Muslims are not even comfortable being around alcohol.

I will never forget a story told by our good friend, Dr. Abbas Alikhan, that took place during his ten year pursuit of his PhD degree from Penn State University. I have never laughed so hard in my entire life as I did when he recounted his experience. One day, Dr. Abbas had decided to go to the Penn State football game. And, of course, what goes better with a football game in America than an ice-cold beer? As the story goes, the man in the bleachers behind Dr. Abbas was indulging in a cold brew when, in his excitement over a touchdown, he dropped his beer bottle. Unfortunately it rolled directly under Dr. Abbas' seat. Although it was obvious the man had already had too much beer, he was anxious to reclaim his bottle of beer. He leaned forward and ask Dr. Abbas to retrieve his beer. The inebriated fan had no way of knowing the man to whom he was speaking was a devout Muslim, who was not about to even touch the beer bottle! Trying to avoid a scene, Dr. Abbas thought and thought, hoping to think of a gentle way of informing the tipsy man that he could not give his beer back to him. Dr. Abbas realized he could not simply turn around and tell a drunken fan, a big drunken fan - - "No!".

Finally, Dr. Abbas reached for his handkerchief, folded it neatly around the neck of the bottle and quickly, delicately, and without ever actually touching the bottle, handed it back to the appreciative man,[49] who by now had forgotten the football game completely.

Although Dr. Abbas was bothered by the beer bottle incident when it took place, he now looks back on

---

[49] Dr. Abbas was unaware at the time that touching the alcohol was not the only problem. Islam says you should not encourage or assist anyone to commit a sin. Therefore, had Dr. Abbas known this fact, he would have been unable to return the beer bottle at all.

it and tells his story, able to see the humor of the whole affair. In fact, he is able to look back on the incident and actually laugh - - hard!

My visits to Kuwait have provided me a unique opportunity to not only understand the basic principles of Islam, but also to experience the dramatic impact these religious beliefs have on individuals and every-day life in Kuwait. A trip to Kuwait without learning about Islam would be unenlightened, like a day at the beach - - without sunshine.

6

RULING THE EMIRATE

Government for the People, for the People, and for the People

Lee R. Lambert

"My experience in government is that when things are non-controversial and beautifully coordinated, there is not much going on."

John Fitzgerald Kennedy

Kuwait has proven itself to be one of the most progressive and enlightened Arabic countries in the world. Since becoming independent in 1961, this small emirate has established, among other things, remarkable centers for education, a sophisticated health care system, and one of the world's most respected social welfare programs.

These are just a few of the contributions made to the Kuwaiti quality of life by a government whose critics can be heard describing it as a self-serving absolute monarchy. My family and I have been in Kuwait many times, and we have personally observed the living conditions and broad range of benefits available in Kuwait (with few exceptions these benefits are available to Kuwaitis and foreigners alike). We have spoken with hundreds of Kuwaitis and immigrants about the long list of free services provided to the Kuwait population by the various Ministries of the State of Kuwait. As a result of our personal observations and discussions, we would suggest that the critics of the current form of government in Kuwait should give credit where it is due and admit that, at least, His Highness the Amir, Sheikh Al-Ahmed Al-Jaber Al-Sabah and Crown Prince, Sheikh Saad Al-Abdulla Al-Salem Al-Sabah and their government hold the interests and happiness of their people in high regard.

The Constitution of the State of Kuwait, which was ratified on November 11, 1962, clearly states in Article 4, "Kuwait is a Hereditary Emirate, the succession to which shall be in the descendents of the late Mubarak Al-Sabah." Further in Kuwait's constitution, Article 6 states, "The system of Government in Kuwait shall be democratic, under which sovereignty resides in the people, the source of all powers." The governmental form is very similar to the Constitutional Monarch system used in Great Britain in which there is a Royal Family and an independent Parliament. However, in Kuwait, the Amir, in consultation with his Cabinet of Ministers, retains considerably more legislative authority than the head of Great Britain's Royal Family. If Kuwait's Constitution is followed exactly as written, with the National Assembly[50] in place and functioning as defined, it is unlikely that anyone could deny that a form of democracy is in place and that Kuwait is in no way an absolute monarchy.

However, in two instances when the National Assembly was dissolved by the Amir,[51] the drastic action drew complaints from critics of Kuwait's government. Kuwait's Constitution provides one of the most thoroughly developed and respected government

---

[50] Kuwait's National Assembly consists of 50 elected members who receive KD750 ($2,550) monthly and serve a four-year term. Each National Assembly session lasts eight months with twice-a-week, four-hour meetings as a minimum.

[51] The authority to dissolve the Kuwaiti National Assembly is granted to the Amir in Article 107 of the Constitution of the State of Kuwait which states, "The Amir may dissolve the National Assembly by a decree in which the reasons for the dissolution shall be indicated."

founding documents in the Arab world. Strict adherence to the Kuwait Constitution is a high priority, especially when it concerns the National Assembly, specific legislative duties, and limits of authority. Each time the National Assembly was dissolved, the decision was made for what the Amir firmly believed were the best interests of Kuwait. Each time the decision was made only after investigating all possible alternatives. Based on my personal observations and conversations the majority of the Kuwaitis seem to be relatively satisfied with their lifestyles, whether or not the National Assembly is in operation.

The dissolutions of the Kuwaiti National Assembly occurred in 1976 and again in 1986. Both times this drastic action came as a result of a high degree of deteriorating political conditions throughout the Gulf region, threats to Kuwait's national security, including bombings and assassination attempts, and increased tension between the legislative and executive branches of government. This tension led to a lack of progress and a significant increase in non-productive political bickering. Prior to the initial dissolution in 1976, Kuwait's National Assembly functioned extremely well and established a strong record of accomplishment, while at the same time becoming the model for a balanced, effective governmental structure among the Arab nations. Following both National Assembly dissolutions, elections were held, and the National Assembly was reinstated.

In the Middle East it is common in times of tension and internal disagreement for outside interests to assert their influence and attempt to disrupt, or even replace existing governmental structures with a form of government beneficial to these outside interests. For example, some say Kuwait's internal difficulties in the late 1980s were interpreted by Iraq's Saddam Hussein as strong opposition against the ruling Al-Sabah family, an opposition that he thought would enable him to easily annex Kuwait for Iraq. Hussein could not have been more wrong, as he quickly learned in the first few days of his army's occupation of Kuwait. In reality, Kuwait's internal opposition was purely a national matter reflecting different views on reforms in Kuwait and in no way seriously challenging the legitimacy of the Kuwait ruling family's control. In fact, since 1756, the history of the reign of the Al-Sabah family shows there has been an essentially unwavering loyalty from the Kuwaiti people they have served. Considering the growth, prosperity, and overall quality of life made possible by the Al-Sabah government, it is not difficult to believe that the present Amir, as well as those who have preceded him, conducts himself in a way that exemplifies true governing "for the people."

Certainly, just as an American President is subject to second-guessing, some of the Kuwaiti Amir's decisions may be challenged, and eventually these issues will be resolved. But it is difficult for me to substantiate opposition's claims of self-serving corruption, misuse of Kuwait's financial resources, and a disregard for the best interests of the Kuwaiti people. In fact, it is far easier to believe that no alternative government, monarchy or not, could have done a better job of providing for the current and future needs of the country and its people.

Exactly how has the Al-Sabah government provided for the many needs of its people? The implementation of one of the world's leading educational systems, as well as the government's development and management of Kuwait's economic programs,will be thoroughly discussed in Chapters 8 and 9, however,

there are many other important and trend-setting programs and services provided by the government for its
people that are worthy of mention here.

The government-sponsored health care that is
available free of charge to anyone living in Kuwait
(both citizens and foreign residents) has established a
standard for consistent, high-quality medical care in
the Middle East. In fact, Kuwait's health care services
can be compared favorably with those of any country in
the world operating within a socialized or national
health care environment. The Kuwait Ministry of
Health's objective has been clearly stated, ". . . health for
all before the year 2000." To insure that this objective is
accomplished, the government has included the Kuwaiti health sector among its top priority areas, target-
ing massive sums of money for hospitals, clinics, and
the most modern and specialized equipment to be used
by professionals trained in the finest medical facilities
in the world.

This dedication to the people's health can be
further confirmed by comparing the budget devoted to
this sector with other sectors in the Kuwaiti governmental process. Only the Ministry of Public Works and
the Ministry of Education are allocated more financial
resources than the Ministry of Health. Health-care-re-
lated spending in Kuwait has grown from a level of
about KD10 million ($34 million) in 1961 to more than
KD200 million ($680 million) in 1989.

Stated in a different way, the focus on health care
in Kuwait is evident in the recent improvement in facilities dedicated to administering care to the ill, as well as
providing preventative health care to the well. The
number of hospitals and hospital beds has increased
dramatically from 1962 levels of twelve and 3,000.
There are currently seventeen fully staffed and

equipped hospitals in Kuwait providing nearly 6,000 beds for those in need of medical treatment.

The biggest advancement in dedicated medical facilities has been in the area of preventative health care. While essentially no facilities or services were available in 1961, there are now twenty-five centers whose only function is to see to the prevention needs of the Kuwaiti residents. Dental care is also provided free of charge, and the number of dental clinics funded by the government has reached 160 nationwide, in comparison to only 23 dental clinics in 1962.

While buildings and equipment are one measure of the government's interest in the area of health care, a better yardstick may be the stunning increase in the number of health care professionals employed by Kuwait. According to the latest government statistics (1986), the total number of health care professionals serving Kuwaiti health care needs is 12,227, compared to only 2,459 at the time of independence in 1961. Doctors and nurses are the major contributors to this dramatic increase. Kuwait currently has over 2,500 fully trained doctors and more than 7,000 qualified nurses, the majority of whom are foreigners employed by the Kuwaiti government. These numbers were substantially reduced as a result of the Iraqi occupation of Kuwait; however, it is expected that over the period of the next few years many of these foreign professionals will return.

Although the government provides free health care to all Kuwait residents, a small private medical sector has enjoyed success in providing service to those in Kuwait who, for one reason or another, are not satisfied with the national health care system. Recognizing its contribution to improving the country's health care services, the government encourages this private sector. Currently there are about 300 private doctors and 700 private nurses working in Kuwait at several private clinics and hospitals, most of which are located in and around Kuwait City.

The Kuwaiti government also provides additional support to those patients who have special medical needs that cannot be satisfied by the services and personnel currently available within Kuwait. Under these special circumstances, a patient (or his family) can seek the best possible medical treatment for his particular ailment anywhere in the world, and the government will pay the majority of the expense for this specialized care. America and Great Britain are the most frequent destinations for this special medical treatment.

As Kuwait's population began to grow after 1961, the government anticipated the need for medical services to be decentralized and geographically distributed to enable the people, no matter where they lived, to have easy access to the care they needed. As a result of this foresight, the country was divided into six health-care areas, each with its own independent, full-service health-care capabilities. This plan calls for each area to have facilities and staff to service a minimum of 300,000 people, thus making high quality health care readily accessible to the entire population of Kuwait.

Have the health care policies enacted by the Kuwaiti government been successful? Two of the best indicators of the quality and availability of health care are mortality rate and life expectancy at birth. Kuwait's current mortality rate is among the lowest in the world at four per thousand - down from eight per thousand in 1965. This figure compares favorably to the United States' rate of nine per thousand and Great Britain's rate of twelve per thousand. In the Arab world, Egypt, Jordan, and Saudi Arabia have rates of ten, eight, and nine per thousand, respectively.

Also, Kuwait is second only to the industrialized Western nations in the category of life expectancy. While the West has seen dramatic improvement in life expectancy, from 68 years for a male child and 74 years for a female child born in 1965 to 74 years and 80 years for those born in the late 1980s, Kuwait's comparative information also shows a marked improvement. Kuwaiti males born today can expect to live to the age of 69, an additional eight years over the 1965 expectation of 61 years, while Kuwaiti females have an improved life expectancy of ten years, from 64 to 74 years during the same time frame. If these statistical samples are valid indicators, the evidence of success in the government-funded health care system cannot be disputed.

The Gulf war had a devastating effect upon the Kuwaiti medical system, as the occupying Iraqi army not only caused severe structural damage to medical facilities but also removed most of the sophisticated medical equipment, shipping it to Baghdad. The challenge facing the Kuwaiti government in the next several years, then, will be to re-establish the health services sector to its original, fully functioning condition. This challenge is formidable and will require the use of innovative approaches to acquire the proper equipment and to convince large numbers of the properly qualified foreign medical staff to return to Kuwait, thus assuring Kuwait residents that they will be able to receive the exceptional medical care to which they have become accustomed.

Anyone who has listened to the on-going debate in the United States concerning our Social Security system can appreciate the difficulties associated with developing, implementing, and finally funding a stable and secure process for caring for a nation's senior citizens and those "special case" individuals who, for one reason or another, cannot function effectively within the basic societal structure.

Kuwait's challenges in this area are exactly the same as those facing the government of the United States, but on a much smaller scale in regard to the number of people and the amount of money involved.

The Kuwaiti government takes considerable pride in its present social security system. It rightly claims that it compares favorably with similar systems developed throughout the world, including that of the United States. As in most countries, Kuwait's social security system is focused on providing for the care of senior citizens through the payment of pension funds, as well as taking care of the poor, mentally impaired, or physically handicapped.

In 1962, Kuwait established the Social Security Public Authority as the embodiment of Article 11 of the Constitution of the State of Kuwait, which reads, "The State ensures aid for citizens in old age, sickness, or inability to work. It also provides them with services of social security, social, and medical care."

In the beginning, Kuwait's social security system was totally funded by the government and was available only to those working in the areas of civil service and the military. In 1981, however, voluntary participation in the system was offered to all Kuwaiti citizens working in Kuwait. This voluntary option remained available until 1986 when the government made participation in the social security system mandatory for all Kuwaiti citizens working in Kuwait, including anyone who is self-employed or earns a living through involvement in Kuwaiti business or trade.

Kuwait's social security system is currently financed through monthly deductions from the salaries of Kuwaiti workers. The workers contribute five percent of their income and employers match it. The government contribution is another ten percent, bringing the total social security revenue contribution per individual worker to twenty percent of the total salary earned. Participants in Kuwait's social security system can begin to receive benefits after 20 years of contribution by a male and 15 years by a female.

The amount collected for each Kuwaiti worker is comparable to the American worker's total contribution of fifteen percent (7.5 from employee and 7.5 from employer) of the first $53,000 earned in 1991. Social security is an expensive program, and the cost of maintaining this critical service must be passed on to the workers in Kuwait, as they are in America. However, since the worker's payments to Kuwait's social security system are essentially the only form of tax levied upon Kuwaiti workers, not many complaints are lodged.

Generally speaking, the services, benefits, and restrictions for Kuwait's social security system are very similar to those in the United States. It is a comprehensive system that is positioned to provide long-term benefits for all Kuwaiti residents who have participated in and contributed to the system's financing. In fact, by 1985, nearly 10,000 families in Kuwait had received some social security-related assistance at a cost to the system of almost KD80 million ($275 million).

In a related area, the Kuwaiti government has given much attention and devoted a great deal of its resources to a general category referred to as social services. These government-supported services are intended to provide citizens with benefits and opportunities that will raise the economic and social standards of the Kuwait society. Most of the social services are designed to provide services to two specific classifications of the Kuwait population: the poor and those either physically or mentally disadvantaged. The first category includes programs targeted to assist the elderly, widowed, orphaned, ill, and divorced. For the second group the government provides home services for the handicapped and special vocational training for those who are able to work in a limited capacity. To date, approximately 24,000 Kuwait citizens have benefited from this government assistance, which averages over KD1.5 million ($5 million) annually.

It took only one visit for us to realize how strongly the Kuwaiti people and their leaders feel about taking care of members of their society who have been stricken with illness or other unfortunate circumstances beyond their control. The government provides the programs and the financial assistance, while family and friends provide the love and personal support that is so vitally important. Loyalty and devotion to family and friends are Kuwaiti traits that transcend political and financial barriers and are two of the characteristics we find most admirable about Kuwait's society.

In keeping with its focus on preventative health care, the Kuwaiti government has chosen to stress physical fitness as part of the Kuwaiti educational experience. An extensive system of parks and sports centers has been developed to accommodate the need for organized and competitive athletics, as well as simple recreational sports. Although we did not observe in Kuwait the level of preoccupation and near obsession with sports that is prevalent in the United States, it is clear that sports of all kinds are becoming an integral part of Kuwaiti society. This rapid expansion of interest and participation in sports is due in large part to the exposure to all types of sporting endeavors that the well-traveled Kuwaiti students and vacationers have experienced during the past fifteen years.

Once again the pro-active government of Kuwait has anticipated this new sporting trend. In 1962 only one sporting club (similar to American health clubs), which provided individual members the opportunity to become athletically active, existed in Kuwait with only two sports federations representing team sports. Today, approximately 65,000 Kuwait residents participate in 20 sporting clubs and 14 federations. Facilities which have been developed using government support include six world-class sports stadiums, each with a capacity of 25,000 fans. The government's contribution to the on-going sports and physical fitness craze has reached nearly KD15 million ($51 million), and a separate investment of more than KD500,000 ($1.7 million), has been made in the Kuwaiti Olympic Committee.

Kuwait's soccer team has been particularly successful, reaching the final rounds of both the Olympics and the World Cup. Swimming and equestrian competitors have also achieved considerable success, representing Kuwait in both Arab and Asian competitions. Kuwait's equestrian team captured the gold, silver, and bronze medals in the Asian Games and, as host nation, won the Fifth Arab Equestrian Championships in 1985. The Junior Swim Team captured 19 medals in the Asian Championships. America has played an important role in the steady growth in number, popularity, and quality of the Kuwaiti sports activities, thanks to the Kuwaiti government investing in expert coaches and critical organizational advice.

Perhaps the most visible evidence of the government's commitment to providing Kuwaitis with a peaceful, relaxing, and enjoyable lifestyle is the fabulous Water Front Project. Beginning at the Kuwait Towers and stretching nearly fifteen miles along the shore of the Arabian Gulf is a beautifully developed park that literally left us staring in amazement. The park combines attractive brick and concrete walkways running its entire length with small concession areas and rest facilities sprinkled generously along the way. Mini-playgrounds with the latest equipment are strategically positioned to insure that children of all ages will have something to keep them occupied.

The soft sand beach has been carefully leveled and is kept meticulously clean for the thousands of Kuwaiti residents, who regularly bring the entire family to the seashore to sit, talk, and eat. Because of the strict Islamic dress code, which requires extreme modesty, we have never seen anyone swimming at this beach, although Kuwaitis do enjoy swimming, and private facilities provide separate male and female pools for their use. However, an occasional non-Kuwaiti can be seen dressed in shorts, walking in the water in hopes of getting some relief from the exceptionally hot summer season.

The Water Front is well lighted, and it is not unusual to find the walkways filled to capacity at midnight, as Kuwaitis engage in their favorite pastimes - - walking and socializing with friends and family. The government has also provided people numerous other parks and recreational facilities throughout Kuwait, but we found the Water Front Project to be the most outstanding example of the government's commitment to invest its resources in projects that directly benefit the people. We were relieved to learn that the damage to the Water Front during the Iraqi invasion and occupation was not extensive and that within a few weeks, the crowds were seen once again strolling along its brick walkways.

The list of government sponsored or supported

programs, activities, services, and facilities for the Kuwaiti people is almost endless. Despite several years of financial instability resulting from the downward trend in world oil prices, the government has continued to demonstrate its commitment to providing for the needs and desires of its people.

The Kuwaiti government places high priority on satisfying other needs of its people related to housing, water, and electricity.

In the housing category, the government's objective is clear: provide a home for every Kuwaiti citizen and his family. Dozens of studies, including one done in America, have indicated that owning a home is key to an individual's physical and psychological health. A home provides shelter, security, peace of mind, and stability. These same studies have made a direct link between ownership of a comfortable home and increased rates of productivity - - another important issue on the Kuwaiti government's list of concerns.

Therefore, the Kuwaiti government has developed a comprehensive housing plan and remains fully committed to providing completed, low- cost houses on government-developed lots, as well as 20-year, interest-free loans to build houses on a lot of the individual's choice, and subsidized temporary housing, while waiting for the permanent residence to be completed.

We have seen concrete evidence (literally) of the tremendous activity in home construction being undertaken in Kuwait. Every part of Kuwait City we visited, every suburb we drove through, had its own government-supported housing development in various stages of completion. In each of these areas, the development had been carefully planned to include all of the necessary social and public services and amenities, such as parks, shopping centers and garbage collection.

By the end of the 1980s, the Kuwaiti government had already completed and turned over more than 50,000 houses to its citizens in Kuwait City, Jahra, Hawalli, Al-Farwaniya, and Ahmadi. Despite the tremendous resources the government has devoted to this housing effort, nearly 50,000 more houses are needed just to fill the requirements which afford housing to all 21-year-old, married male Kuwaiti citizens.

Those first-time Kuwaiti home-owners fortunate enough to own their own property, or those who are wealthy enough to buy land, are still eligible to receive assistance from the government, usually in the form of low, or no interest loans with liberal repayment schedules. These privately constructed homes are generally much larger and significantly more elaborate than the standard government-issue house. This private construction approach has accounted for more than 200,000 houses completed and occupied by Kuwaiti citizens since 1962.

As a result of the lack of large quantities of high quality land suited for housing development, it is not unusual to see entire families located in the same area, with each family member building his own house on the family owned property. We know several families who have their brothers, parents, uncles, and cousins all living next door to one another in their private homes. On one of our trips to Kuwait we visited the nearly completed house of a friend from the Kuwait Institute for Scientific Research (KISR), who also happened to be the brother of a former Kuwaiti Minister. It was a beautiful, two-story house with a full basement, including quarters for household help and an extensive working kitchen. This University of Southern California graduate, his wife, and three children had been waiting for the new home for almost seven years. As we prepared to leave at the conclusion of our tour, my friend pointed to several of the already-occupied homes along the street and proudly indicated that all belonged to members of his family.

We think that the economics of finding land and building a home in Kuwait provides a good excuse for keeping large families close to each other. However, we also think, from the close ties we have observed between Kuwaiti families, that even if economics and scarcity of land were not factors, families would make every attempt to live as close to each other as possible.

Although the government's focus is clearly on providing a house for every Kuwaiti citizen, it has not overlooked the critical needs of the immigrant labor force. Working with the private sector, the government has attempted to insure that all those who come to Kuwait to live and work have adequate and affordable housing available to them and their families. To assure this supply of housing for the important immigrant labor force, the government has encouraged Kuwaiti companies to include housing arrangements as part of the standard immigrant labor contract.

Normally, foreigners are not permitted to own property in Kuwait. In some very special cases, however, foreigners (generally citizens of the Gulf Cooperation Council countries) are allowed to own property in Kuwait. Generally this "outside" ownership is accomplished through some involvement of the foreigner's private shareholding company, which, by law, must have some Kuwaiti citizen ownership and participation.[52]

---

[52] The Gulf Cooperation Council (GCC) was formed in 1981 by five Gulf States (Kuwait, Oman, Qatar, Bahrain, United Arab Emirates) and Saudi Arabia in reaction to Iran's desire to expand its Islamic Revolution beyond its boarders. The purpose of the GCC is to coordinate planning of political, social, economic and defense matters. It is based in Riyadh, Saudi Arabia.

As for the importance of fresh water and electricity, it is clear that without the availability of reliable and affordable water and electricity, the people of Kuwait would be unable to enjoy many of the benefits which accompany the wealth and the modernization of the country.

The Al-Sabah led government is dedicated to constantly improving the services to the people in these two critical areas. The first electrical generation plant in Kuwait was commissioned in 1952 with a production capacity of only 750 kw (.75 mega watt). This first oil-fired Kuwait power plant seemed extremely small when compared to the estimated 7,000,000kw (7,000 mega watt) generation capacity of America's hydroelectric plant at Ground Coulee Station, but it was a major achievement for Kuwait and provided a new level of electrical service to the Kuwaiti people.

The government now boasts the completion of four more power generation plants and a total production capacity of over 7,000 mega watts. In conjunction with the expansion of production capability came the design and construction of adequate distribution systems to get the power to users. These electrical distribution systems are constantly being improved and expanded by the Ministry of Electricity and Water.

Currently Kuwait has nearly 10,000 miles of underground cable and 1,500 miles of overhead power lines serving consumers who have ignored any noticeable conservation while registering the highest per capita consumption rate in the world.[53] All of the new construction has incorporated the latest underground

---

[53] Kuwait ranks 11th in the world in per capita in electrical power consumption at 8,663 kilowatt hours. The United States is 7th (10,781), while Norway is 1st (24,777). The U.S. cost per kilowatt hour is $.078 for residential use and $.048 for industrial users.

technology to improve the appearance and safety associated with such an extensive power distribution
system.

While the government does not provide its
people with free electricity, generous subsidies have
kept the cost to consumers very low. Domestic consumers pay approximately two fils ($.07) per kilowatt hour
of consumption, while industrial users incur a cost of
only one fil ($.034) for the same usage. The importance
of the Kuwaiti government contribution is easily quantified when comparing the rates charged to users with
the actual cost to produce and distribute the electricity,
which is around 30 fills ($1.00) per kilowatt hour.

In 1907 Kuwait initiated its first fresh water
transportation endeavor. As you can imagine, this was
a slow time-consuming process. Kuwait utilized 49
large *dhows* (boats) to carry 80,000 gallons of fresh water
from Shatt Al-Arab in Iraq to Kuwait. By 1953 the
government had commissioned its first desalination
plant, which was capable of producing one million
gallons of fresh water each day to meet the needs of the
rapidly growing oil industry.

The government has never lost sight of the importance of fresh water. Currently Kuwait's five distil-
lation plants have a total daily production capacity of
over 200 million gallons. Once delivered to houses by a
huge fleet of trucks, today's modern distribution system is comprised of a complex underground piping
system that reaches the majority of the homes and industrial sites in Kuwait.

The production and distribution capacity that
has been developed by the government is capable of
providing a daily surplus of almost 110 million gallons.
However, even with this huge surplus production capacity, the government is working hard to develop and

implement a realistic conservation program to anticipate the long term needs for fresh water. Part of that
conservation strategy includes a well-planned ration-
ing scheme and restricted use of the precious fresh
water - - estimated at 50 billion gallons of reserves - - in
the Rawdhatain and Um Al-Aish underground
reservoirs.

Almost fifty percent of the local drinking water
consumption need is met by the output of the Al-
Rawdhatain bottling plant, located about sixty miles
north of Kuwait City with an annual production capacity of three million gallons. The balance of the bottled
mineral water is imported from vendors throughout the
world.

As a final means on minimizing the country's
waste of drinking quality distilled water, the Kuwaiti
government has enthusiastically promoted the expansion of the use of huge quantities of underground
brackish (slightly salty and not fit to drink) water as a
supplement. This brackish water utilization reached a
total of twenty-two billion gallons last year as it was
used almost exclusively for irrigation, street cleaning
and watering livestock. The government has financed a
completely separate network of piping to carry the
large volumes of brackish water from five different
locations to the Kuwaiti consumer.

Ministers with whom I have spoken share their
government's sincere and unselfish devotion to developing and implementing programs and policies that are
in the best long-term interests of Kuwait and its people.
We found these same Ministers working long hours in
the office and regularly found them working at home or
attending a *diwaniya* to obtain a better understanding
of the people's attitudes and desires so they could
more effectively represent the people in establishing

government programs and policies.

The subject of guaranteed employment for all Kuwaitis is worthy of mention when speaking of beneficial Kuwaiti government programs. Although we were told technically there is no government guarantee that all Kuwaitis will have a job, in practice the net effect is almost the same. The government clearly states that any Kuwaiti willing and able to work will be given first priority in the distribution of jobs within the country. Since Kuwait relies so heavily on immigrant labor in all segments of the society - - professional, vocational, and manual - - it quickly becomes obvious that any able bodied Kuwaiti could always secure a job.

Kuwaitis working in the government sector, in one of the Ministries or related government areas, are paid a base rate plus additional compensation for higher education, special employment fields, and marriage. The base salary for an unmarried Kuwaiti with a college degree is KD360 ($1,225) per month. A Kuwaiti with only a high school diploma earns substantially less with a base salary of KD225 ($765) each month. In the event of marriage, the base salaries are increased by KD170 ($578) and KD150 ($510) per month respectively. Additional increases are provided for those who enter critical professional areas such as education, engineering, medicine, or law.[54] The working hours for most government employees are liberal, with a normal schedule of 7 a.m. to 1p.m., and all government workers must work a minimum of 38 hours each week.

In the private sector, salaries can vary significantly, and the normal working day is 8 a.m. to 5 p.m., although many companies have a "split" schedule,

---

[54] All Kuwaiti citizens received an across-the-board 25% salary increase after the Gulf War ended.

allowing for a break during the severe heat of the afternoon. The Kuwaiti government is constantly examining
ways to encourage more and more private employment
in order to decrease the high level of government dependency that currently exists.

There is a theory about Third World rulers and
how they are able to obtain the consent of those they
govern. This theory maintains that Third World rulers
obtain and retain the consent of their people in one, or
a combination, of three ways. The first is to obtain
consent through coercion and terror, an example being
Iraq's President, Saddam Hussein, also referred to as
the Butcher of Baghdad. The second method is to avoid
criticism by blaming everything that goes wrong on
some external force over which the ruler has no direct
control. In many Arab countries, for example, the diver-
sionary blame usually is thrown on Israel. Finally, the
third tactic suggested by this theory is for the governing
entity to reward the people being governed as well as it
can for as long as it can.

As far as I could see during our times in Kuwait,
the first and second methods mentioned above have no
applicability. Kuwait has intentionally developed and
maintained a very small military (20,000 troops), which
clearly eliminates the first approach, and the only significant problems or concerns Kuwait has had in recent
years have been caused by Iraq and Iran,[55] not Israel.
That leaves the third method for serious consideration.

I am not in a position to judge whether the motive behind the government's incredibly diverse and

---

[55] Originally known as Persia, Iran took on its new identity in 1935.
Contrary to most American beliefs, Iran is not an Arab nation. It is,
however, a Muslim state and the majority of its 43 million people are
members of the Shiite sect (the Persians were once Sunni Muslims, but
converted to Shiite enmass during the 1400s). The official language of Iran
is Farsi - - not Arabic.

sustained level of service to the people of Kuwait has been to placate the people, thus allowing the Al-Sabah reign to continue unbroken, or if these endowments to society have come as a result of an honest and sincere dedication to serving Kuwait and its people.

There is evidence, especially in the case of its pre-invasion relationship with Iraq, suggesting that the Kuwaiti government has occasionally made large payments (blackmail disguised as a loan) to Iraq in order to insure Kuwaiti citizens remain free from the threats and intimidation from its much stronger, more ambitious neighbor. However, I saw no evidence that this "buy-'em-off" tactic has ever been utilized by the Kuwait government on its own citizens.

Whatever the motivation and justification behind the very benevolent policies of the Al-Sabah government over the years, and regardless of the "game" this long line of rulers may have been playing in Kuwait, two facts cannot be disputed: they play it very well, and the Kuwaiti people always seem to be the winners.[56]

---

[56] Following the Gulf War the Kuwaiti Government forgave all consumer loans (cars, boats, furniture etc.), and all home loans (up to a maximum of KD 54,000 0r $184,000). The Government also increased Kuwaiti workers' salaries by 25% and paid each Kuwaiti family a lump sum to aid in their personal recovery from the effects of the Gulf War.

7

MAINTAINING LAW AND ORDER

Dedicated to the Pursuit of Justice

Lee R. Lambert

*"It is the spirit and not the form of the law
that keeps justice alive."*

Chief Justice Earl Warren

Thankfully, we cannot cite any personal experience with the Kuwaiti legal system. But, like most Westerners, we have heard frightening stories about how people in Islamic cultures are punished with undue severity for committing a relatively minor crime such as petty theft. Cases of persons having their right hand[57] cut off for stealing or being publicly flogged for eating during the observance of Ramadan have been widely reported in the Western press. We were relieved, therefore, when our research into Kuwait's legal system failed to uncover a single case. Instead, we found a comprehensive and sophisticated legal system supported by a hierarchy of courts structured to deal with a variety of cases of a civil, commercial, personal, and criminal nature. Likewise, we found adequate penal facilities to house persons who had been found guilty of crimes requiring detention. These prisons include the

---

[57] In Arab cultures it is thought that the left hand is to be used for bathroom duties and cleaning oneself. Eating with the left hand is generally considered unsanitary and disgraceful. Therefore a punishment of the loss of the right hand has a particular stigma attached to it.

central prison in Kuwait City, a secondary prison in Doha, a women's prison, and a separate juvenile detention facility. Additionally, each police station in the five political governorates has a jail available for the temporary retention of prisoners awaiting trial, and there is also a separate military prison.

The Kuwait legal system is founded on French legal principals, as interpreted and implemented in Egypt.[58] However, Islamic Law (*Sharia*)[59] also plays a significant role in determining how the French law is implemented or interpreted for Kuwait's application. Kuwait's Ministry of Islamic Affairs is currently involved in the production of a comprehensive modern Encyclopedia of Islamic Law. This vital seminal work is aimed at interpreting Islamic Law, according to the recorded teachings of Muhammad in the Koran, in a perspective that addresses the environment and requirements of the 20th century. Kuwait is exercising extreme care in using only the most up-to-date methods to ensure accuracy and authenticity of the information on Islamic Law. When completed, this impressive set of reference documentation will include over 5,000 Islamic legal terms that will be approved by an official Expert Committee comprised of professors from the Faculty of Sharia and advisors from the Ministry of Justice. As of 1992, more than half of the anticipated 20 volume set has been completed.

The most apparent difference between existing

---

[58] Egypt's legal system operates under the Napoleonic (French) code of justice, but the government is under constant pressure to adopt the Islamic legal system (*Sharia*).

[59] *Sharia's* Arabic translation is, "the road to the watering place," or "the clear path to be followed," and is interpreted to mean, "the path of God." The *Sharia* consists of all God's commandments relating to human activities. It prescribes regulations for worship and ritual and for political and legal activities.

Kuwaiti law and the more traditional, ancient Islamic Law is in the types and methods of punishment inflicted upon convicted law breakers. For example, in the case of someone found guilty of consuming alcohol in Kuwait, Islamic Law calls for the guilty person to receive 80 flogs. The punishment for the same offense under the Kuwaiti French-based system is a maximum of six months in prison. Surprisingly, in some instances, the current system's punishment is far more severe than that required under Islamic Law. An individual who is apprehended for violation of the Ramadan ban on food, drink, and smoking during daylight hours provides a good case in point. In fact, under Islamic Law, there is no required punishment for this crime, whereas under current Kuwaiti law, the courts can hand out a maximum sentence of one month imprisonment and/or a KD100 ($340) fine. The Ramadan restrictions in Kuwait apply to Muslims and non-Muslims alike, and visitors to Kuwait can expect little sympathy if they attempt to use ignorance as an excuse for failure to comply. Although we have never been in Kuwait during Ramadan, we have heard many stories about foreigners who have found themselves in jail for violating the ban on eating, drinking, or smoking in public. Generally, these people have not been detained long, but their stay in jail was long enough, and the fine big enough, to clearly demonstrate the seriousness of the Kuwaiti Law concerning Ramadan restrictions.

Moral crimes, which comprise only a small portion of the Kuwaiti court caseload each year, provide the most stark contrast between Islamic Law and Kuwait's French based system. Under traditional Islamic Law a married man or woman convicted of adultery is to be stoned to death, while an unmarried man or woman found guilty of the same offense is publicly flogged. Under the Kuwaiti system, the same crime calls for five years imprisonment or a 5,000 Rupees ($200) fine in the case of the convicted married person and three-years imprisonment or a 3,000 Rupees ($115) fine in case of a convicted unmarried person. The reference to the Indian Rupee currency as the method of payment for fines reflects written law that has not been revised since Kuwait discontinued using the Rupee in 1961, replacing it with the Kuwaiti Dinar as the official currency of the State of Kuwait.[60]

For major crimes such as theft, rape, murder, and selling drugs, the Kuwaiti legal system is committed to handing out severe punishments. Nevertheless, Kuwaiti judges are able to temper their decisions based on the unique circumstances surrounding each case, and the mandatory sentences allow flexibility to accommodate any special conditions. For example, a convicted thief can receive a maximum of life in prison or a minimum of just two years behind bars. A person found guilty of selling drugs in Kuwait is faced with a possible maximum sentence of fifteen years in prison, but may only serve the minimum of seven years imprisonment.

Murder and rape, two of the most violent and serious crimes in any society, appropriately carry the most severe punishments for those convicted in the Kuwaiti courts. A rapist can expect to spend a minimum of ten years in prison; and, if the circumstances warrant, the maximum punishment option available to the judge

---

[60] The defeat of the Ottoman Empire in World War I resulted in a significant expansion of Kuwait trade with India. One version of how the Indian Rupee became Kuwait's currency suggests that a wealthy Kuwaiti merchant sold a large quantity of pearls to Indian merchants in Indian Rupees. The huge amount of Indian Rupees flooded the Kuwait market and eventually caused other currencies to disappear. The Indian Rupee remained legal tender in Kuwait until 1961 when it was replaced by the current Kuwaiti Dinar.

is execution by hanging. Hanging is also a possibility for the convicted murder, while the minimum punishment for this most heinous of crimes is twenty-five years behind bars. Depending on the particular crime, the Kuwaiti Amir has the option of granting a pardon after the convicted person has served one-third of the prescribed sentence. Parole for convicted felons is considered on a case-by-case basis.

Compared to many Western societies, Kuwait's overall crime rate is low. The latest statistics for murder or attempted murder indicate that fewer than 200 cases a year are brought before Kuwaiti judges.[61]

The reported incidents of rape are so low that separate statistics for this category were not available. However, during our many trips to Kuwait we can remember only two times when we read in local newspapers of someone being arrested on suspicion of committing rape. The majority of the criminal activity in Kuwait, occupying the time of the nearly 6,000 police officers nationwide, is perpetrated by traffic law violators and individuals issuing bad checks.

If a person is accused of a serious crime, the Kuwaiti system has developed a court system that attempts to ensure that the defendant receives a fair and just trial. The basic hierarchy of courts include the First Instance Court, in which one judge deals with the administration of the trial, determining the verdict, and defining the punishment; the Court of Appeals, in which three judges review cases that have been referred

---

[61] According to the New Book of World Rankings (source INTERPOL: International Crime Statistics), Third Edition, Kuwait's current murder rate is 1 in 100,000 population. This rate ranks Kuwait 72nd among 78 countries reported. In comparison, the United States ranked 15th with 8 murders per 100,000 people.

to it for reconsideration; and the Supreme Court, where five judges act as the final review and ultimate decision-making body for all cases not resolved in the Court of Appeals. In addition, there is also a Court of Summary Justice, similar to Small Claims Court in the United States. Cases involving commercial and civil misdemeanors where no more than KD1,000 ($3,400) is involved can be resolved through the Court of Summary Justice. The court's rulings are final if the sum of money awarded is no more than KD500 ($1,700); but, if the sum of money awarded exceeds this amount, either party may appeal the decision to the First Instance Court for reconsideration.

In the Kuwaiti system of justice, there are no juries. Legal advisors - - someone granted authority to make decisions on simple cases - - or judges have the sole responsibility for hearing the evidence and determining the verdict as well as handing out the appropriate sentence. In more serious cases, only a judge listens to the evidence that has been collected by the prosecutor and the defense attorney before making a decision. Often times the accused may not even have the opportunity to face his accusers in court, and the judge is expected to be able to separate fact from fiction as the case is presented. A convicted person does have the option of appeal, providing just cause can be proven.

Kuwaiti courts are very busy, but the majority of the cases concern commercial or business disputes, traffic violations, and personal financial matters. The recent completion of the Grand Courts Complex in the center of Kuwait City has helped improve the speed and efficiency of the Kuwait court system. This massive nine-story (plus two basement levels) building has consolidated all of the previously widely disbursed courts into one location. This impressive structure houses all the Kuwait courts, public prosecution offices, and other associated legal-system operations. It provides fifty-two court rooms, thirty-nine of which are dedicated to the First Instance Court activities.

The existing Kuwaiti legal system is committed to the equal treatment of women before the law. However, judges are given freedom to take into consideration any special circumstances involved in a specific case involving a woman, just as in the case of a male defendant. The woman's prison is usually filled to capacity with the primary offense being some form of minor moral crime. This prison is staffed and operated entirely by women.

A part of Kuwaiti Law that is often not publicized relates to the import of "prohibited" articles or substances. It is forbidden to bring such items as dangerous or illegal drugs, alcohol, fireworks, firearms, or ammunition, pornographic materials, politically subversive materials, pork products, including anything made of pigskin, and any goods from Israel or South Africa into the country. Typically, if a visitor is found to have any of these items upon entering Kuwait, he may advise the Customs Officer, who will simply confiscate the items and send the traveller on his way. However, if a person is suspected of attempting to bring any of these materials into the country purposely for sale or personal use, he may be subject to arrest and prosecution. Kuwait is strictly a prohibition State (absolutely no alcohol is allowed, even in foreign embassies),[62] but some residents of Kuwait and visitors from abroad

---

[62] Kuwait is one of only four Arab nations that remain committed to their anti-alcohol tradition. Absolutely no alcohol can be legally sold or consumed in Kuwait, Saudi Arabia, Qatar and Libya. The treatment of alcohol sales and consumption varies among the other Arab nations and in some instances there are severe restrictions against Arabs purchasing alcohol, while foreigners are permitted.

continue to maintain a black market supply of alcohol for consumption at private social and business functions, almost always conducted in a private home. I have been offered alcohol on several occasions when we have been entertained at someone's home. However, since I do not drink alcohol by personal choice, I have never been in the position of breaking Kuwaiti law.

Consistent with the Kuwaiti-to-non-Kuwaiti population distribution, the latest available statistics indicate that slightly less than forty percent (2,113) of the convicted felons (5,365) during a year in Kuwait are Kuwaiti citizens. In the category of misdemeanor offences, the same ratio exists, as thirty-nine percent (2,237) of the total (5,781) convictions involved natural-born Kuwaitis. These latest statistics also verify the low incidence of crimes in Kuwait. Of the 5,365 felony convictions, only fourteen percent involved physical violence against another person.

Based on personal conversation and recent press coverage, it appears that the Kuwaiti legal system is not necessarily universally admired. Complaints from the Western legal community persist in regard to Kuwait's total reliance on the decision of judges without providing the accused an opportunity to be judged by a jury of his peers.[63] The actual method of conducting trials has also been challenged, including cases when the accused is not present during the trial, or not given an opportunity to face his accusers, and, in some cases,

---

[63] America is often considered to have the most sophisticated and fairly administered legal system in the world, but even its jury-of-peers method is not perfect. The 1992 Los Angeles riots - - the worst in America's history and the cause of nearly $1 billion in property damage and more than 60 people being killed - - were sparked by public outrage over a Simi Valley, California jury's innocent verdict on charges against four Los Angeles police officers accused of using excessive force in making an arrest of an African American.

not even allowed to provide a personal defense testimony. Although these claims are generally accurate, and illustrate the substantial differences from the United States' legal methods, the Kuwaiti system of justice remains one of the most advanced, sophisticated, and fairest in the Arab world.[64]

---

[64] Source material for several portions of this chapter was generously researched and provided by Khaled Al-Tahek, a Kuwaiti lawyer.

8

EMPHASIS ON EDUCATION

Preparing the Next Generation

Lee R. Lambert

*" Education is a social process . . . Education is growth . . .
Education is not a preparation for life; Education is life itself"*

John Dewey

On February 14, 1978, less than two months after assuming the position of the thirteenth ruler of Kuwait, His Highness the Amir Jaber Al-Ahmad Al-Jaber Al-Sabah proclaimed, "The Kuwait of tomorrow belongs to the Kuwait youth, men, and women alike. The country is surging forward to a bright future based on the confidence, will, and determination of its youth." Few would take exception to the Amir's claim, and most Kuwaitis would agree that the conduit for achieving this bright future for Kuwait lies in education.

Since terminating its status as a Great Britain protectorate in 1961, the Kuwait government's unparalleled investment in providing free educational opportunities to its citizens has resulted in an overall Kuwait literacy rate of nearly eighty percent. This figure, by far the highest of any Arab nation, represents a seventy-five percent increase over the 1961 literacy rate of just five percent. Naturally, Kuwait's young people are the major beneficiaries. Kuwait's literacy rate for ten-to-fourteen year olds is ninety-one percent for girls and an astonishing ninety-six percent for boys. This compares favorably with a literacy rate of 95.7 percent for American boys of the same age.

Among other Kuwaitis, however, illiteracy is more common, a situation that the Kuwait government has addressed. Literacy is a very important objective for the Kuwait government, and its eradication is clearly stated and supported by law. To that end, the government, realizing that traditional approaches to general education would not be adequate to meet the needs of all people suffering from illiteracy, especially the older Kuwaiti generation, has established what they call "Illiteracy Centers," where individuals may attend and take advantage of special programs that have been developed to teach reading and writing. Participation at these centers has been on a steady rise with over 30,000 people currently taking part in more than one thousand programs. The Kuwait government employs nearly four thousand teachers to staff these vital centers.

The Kuwaiti educational challenge is being attacked at all levels. Kuwait's schools, universities, and applied colleges have set the standard of excellence for others in the Gulf region for many years. The leaders of Kuwait remain convinced that their substantial investment in public education will pay big dividends as Kuwait enters the turbulent 1990s. Following the Iraqi invasion and the eventual anticipated impact that event will have on the skill and labor mix available in Kuwait, the huge investment Kuwait has made in education would seem almost prophetic in preparing Kuwaitis to assume entry-level management, some middle-management, semi-professional, and semi-skilled jobs previously held by foreigners.

Kuwait, like most other countries in the world, operates a national educational system. That is, the educational process is defined, implemented, and controlled by the State of Kuwait. This total oversight responsibility extends from kindergarten through the higher educational structure of Kuwait University and the various Applied Colleges. Interestingly, the United States is one of the few nations in the world that does not have a national education system; instead, each state is responsible for organizing and regulating its own system of education within some very broad national guidelines.

The majority of states in America have separated the educational process into three classifications: elementary, secondary, and post-secondary. Kuwait has taken a slightly different approach, resulting in four stages of formal, government-sponsored education: kindergarten (voluntary for ages four to six); primary (compulsory for ages six to ten); intermediate (compulsory for ages ten to fourteen); and secondary (elective for ages fourteen to eighteen). Even though compulsory education ends at age fourteen, Kuwait law prohibits young people from working until age sixteen, and the result is that virtually all children attend school until they reach the age of sixteen.

In the United States, school attendance is compulsory in every one of our fifty states, but the mandatory age limit varies from age fourteen to age eighteen, with the majority of states (35) requiring attendance until the age of sixteen.

A big advantage for the Kuwaiti student who desires to obtain the finest possible education is the fact that education is absolutely free from kindergarten through the university level. The student pays for only books and supplies. In some special cases, where a student's home is too far from the school to commute on a regular basis and in the case of Kuwaiti students attending school in other countries, housing is also provided at no charge, and students receive monthly stipends of up to $500. In the case of the students attending schools in other countries, the Kuwaiti government is very strict about the student maintaining acceptable grades (C or above) in order to continue receiving government support. The students progress is closely monitored by a representative of the Ministries of Education and Higher Education in the student's host country.

Primary, intermediate, and secondary students are taught on a segregated basis with separate schools for girls and boys. Kindergarten and university-level instruction is provided on a coeducational basis, although girls and boys generally sit separately within the classrooms. Many foreign private or fee-paying schools[65] are organized in a traditional coeducational format, which essentially reduces the number of classes to be taught therefore reducing the number of qualified foreign teachers that must be recruited and hired by about fifty percent.

All government schools through the secondary level require their students to wear standard uniforms, which vary in style and color depending on the grade level and time of the year. Some of the private schools offer considerably more flexibility in clothing choice for their students.

Kuwait's private schools, although free to develop their own curriculum and hire their own instructors, are inspected regularly and accredited by the Kuwait Ministry of Education. These schools are in high demand and have fees which can range from KD500

---

[65] At the time of the Iraqi invasion there were more than one hundred private schools in Kuwait. These schools were Arab, Indian, American, British, French and German.

($1,700) per year for kindergarten to KD2,000 ($7,000) per year at the high school level. These rather high fees don't seem to prevent the number of applicants competing for selection from increasing each year.

Over the past quarter of a century, the Kuwait educational sector has experienced massive quantitative and qualitative improvements, especially when compared with methods that were in use when the first official all boys school was founded in 1911. At that time, teaching primarily focused on the "three R's"; reading, writing, and 'rithmetic, and the reciting of the Holy Koran. The instruction was provided by male clerics known as *Muttawaa* or *Mullahs*. In a move that seems foreign to the current Kuwaiti environment, the leaders of 1911 imposed an import tax of five percent on all incoming goods and products as the means of financing the new school. The action seemed appropriate at the time, since the main purpose of the school was to prepare writers and bookkeepers to satisfy the needs of the local merchants. Unfortunately, the worldwide depression of 1929 reached as far as Kuwait, and because of economic stagnation and a significant decrease in imported goods to be taxed, the funding to support the school disappeared; and the school, which had been named Mubarakiya School in honor of Mubarak Al-Sabah, the seventh ruler of Kuwait, was closed.

A consistent and structured educational system did not exist in Kuwait until 1936 when a Council of Education was established and the responsibility for education officially shifted from the private sector to the loosely structured government of the times. In 1938 Kuwait opened its first school for girls with 140 students registered and five women teachers. By 1945 there were seventeen schools in Kuwait serving a total enrollment of 3,635.

Dramatic improvements in Kuwait's educational system began in 1947 with large sums of money from the production of oil flowing into the State treasury. Although progress was rapid during the next decade, it wasn't until the Kuwaiti government issued a major Kuwait Educational Plan in 1956 that the real potential of the emirate's educational system began to be realized.

This new educational plan established the four major categories , previously mentioned, that are still being utilized today. This comprehensive plan was extended to include Kuwait University in 1966 and has undergone continuous review and modification to address the current and future educational needs of Kuwait and its people. Kuwait's current approach to planning and executing its educational thrusts is through the on-going development and revision of the educational five-year plan.

Since Kuwait's first educational plan was published in 1956, the improvement in Kuwait's educational system, along with dramatic increases in the student population, has been steady. The Kuwaiti curriculum at all levels is considered to be on a par with most of the world's modern educational systems. Most students who left Kuwait with their parents during the Iraqi crisis were able to enter schools in Great Britain and the United States at the same grade level they had left in Kuwait. Most of the displaced students performed very well, despite the disruption and emotional upheaval, thus, demonstrating the quality of the education they had received in their homeland.

The Kuwaiti government has demonstrated it is prepared to do more than just plan for education. In recent years the Kuwaiti government has earmarked more than ten percent of its total budget for financing

and improving its educational system. This appropria-
tion is exceeded as a budget outlay only by the amount
allocated for operating the electricity and water services of the country. Based on an estimate of nearly
400,000 students attending about 600 state-operated
schools in all grade levels, the government's KD400
million ($1.4 billion) commitment reflects an expendi-
ture of almost $4,000 a year per student.[66]

Prior to the Iraqi invasion, an additional 150,000
students were enrolled in a wide variety of private
schools. In all educational sectors a total of 30,000 teachers and professors were employed to accommodate the
population's educational needs during the 1988-89
school year.

The quality of the Kuwaiti educational experience can be partially attributed to a low student-to-
teacher ratio. Every effort is made to provide one
teacher for every twenty or fewer students in order to
ensure that each student receives the proper individualized attention. This low student-to-teacher ration in
Kuwait provides a stark contrast to our experience in
the United States during recent years, where failing tax
initiatives and a shortage of qualified teachers have
driven our student-to-teacher ratio to about 30:1. The
quality and depth of our educational experience in the
United States will surely be impacted negatively when
each teacher is expected to give personal attention to
such a large number of students.

The overall growth and success of the Kuwaiti
educational system has been impressive, but the rapid

---

[66] According to United States Department of Education, $4,639 per student
is spent on education for primary and secondary pupils. Per capita spending of $771 places the U.S. 7th in the world, while Kuwait ranks 10th with
a per capata spending of $607, Sweden is 1st ($999) and Canada is 2nd
($983).

expansion of Kuwait University has truly been an incredible achievement. In just twenty-six years this institution of higher learning has seen its student population grow from just a few hundred to over 17,000. During the 1988-89 school year the student body at Kuwait University was comprised of about 9,500 female students and 7,500 male students and included approximately 5,000 non-Kuwaiti citizens, all of whom were taught by a faculty of 900 professors and associate professors, of whom nearly 300 are Kuwaiti citizens. Undergraduate degrees are granted in the fields of arts, sciences, education, commerce, law, engineering, Islamic studies, medicine, and health science. The colleges of arts and sciences account for almost fifty percent of the enrollment. All of the sciences, including engineering, are taught in English, while the arts, such as political science, law and literature , are taught entirely in Arabic. The quality of the Kuwait University education can be substantiated through nearly 100-percent acceptance rate of its students applying for admission for advanced degrees from the most highly respected universities in the United States and Great Britain.[67]

The Kuwait Ministry of Education, recognizing the need to provide educational facilities for the families of the vital immigrant labor force, has committed itself to providing a quality education for all school-age children, regardless of nationality. The general enrollment, prior to the Iraqi invasion, in all Kuwaiti government schools averaged about 40-percent non-Kuwaitis. Acceptance criteria for non-Kuwaiti students is deter-

---

[67] Kuwait continues to support a significant number of students seeking their education abroad. In 1992, 1,470 Kuwaitis were working abroad on undergraduate degrees and 102 were involved in graduate programs.

mined on a space-available basis, with priority consideration given as follows: first, citizens of the Gulf Cooperation Council countries; second, Palestinians; third, African Arabs; fourth, all others. In light of the role some Palestinians are alleged to have played in supporting Iraq in its invasion and occupation of Kuwait, its students' priority status will most likely change in the new Kuwait environment.

My experience in Kuwait has shown that children there are not very different from their American counterparts. And they are just as excited to go back to school each year in late August (government school) or mid-September (private school) as are American students - - most would rather have their teeth pulled than go back to school. Children in Kuwait's public schools begin their day at 7:15 a.m . with a salute to the Kuwaiti flag, and they finish their daily studies at 1:00 p.m. Private schools begin slightly later at 7:30 a.m., but classes continue until 2:30 in the afternoon. Lunch is brief and then it's back to the books. This routine is repeated Saturday through Wednesday during the nine-month long school year. Buses are provided for transportation if necessary, but the reliable car pool with mom and dad (sometimes a hired driver) at the wheel has become increasingly popular.

In the 1991-92 school year, Kuwaiti government schools compressed two nine-month school years into one to attempt to recover for the academic year that was essentially lost as a result of the Iraqi invasion and the turmoil and uncertainty that followed the liberation of Kuwait. This attempt to complete two years of material in a single academic year will require the children to attend school for a longer period each day. This two-in-one approach presented a serious problem in the early fall months and late spring months of the school year as the heat in Kuwait reached almost unbearable levels. At the end of July, 1990 all of the Kuwait schools were air-conditioned, but most of the equipment was removed by the Iraqis. Kuwait has been expediting the process of securing and installing the necessary new cooling equipment.

The official language of the State of Kuwait is Arabic, but the unofficial language, and the one often used in the business environment is English. Recognizing the important role the youth of Kuwait will play in the future economics and global politics of their country, the Kuwaiti government has insisted on providing an English curriculum available to all Kuwaiti students beginning in fifth grade. In Kuwait, English is the second language by practice, not by law. The quality of the English language education is quite impressive. I have found it relatively easy to carry on conversations in English with Kuwaiti children who have completed as little as two years of instruction. Children who have an American mother, and there are hundreds of such households, obviously find it much easier to grasp the language and to perfect its use. I am embarrassed to admit that I have been travelling to Kuwait since 1986, and I still cannot understand or speak Arabic as well as these young children comprehend and speak English.

Although Kuwait's educational core curriculum is sound, there is one area where the Kuwaiti approach differs substantially from that being implemented in American schools: the student's physical education. The importance of physical education has begun to be recognized in the Kuwaiti system, but the primary focus remains clearly on academics. Unlike American schools where attending class is often simply an inconvenient prerequisite to participating on a school sponsored competitive athletic team, the Kuwaiti philosophy has resulted in children obtaining their exercise and physical education on a more individualized basis outside the formal school setting. Extracurricular activities are not typically a significant part of a Kuwaiti child's educational experience. However, a wide variety of extracurricular activities is readily available outside the State-operated schools through private facilities, sports clubs, and neighborhood recreation associations. Also many of Kuwait's private schools offer opportunities for their students in a variety of areas, including music, athletics, and dance.

In addition to being thankful for the basic educational opportunities provided by the government, the people of Kuwait also appreciate the fact that their leaders have not overlooked two very special categories: religious instruction and "special" education. Kuwait is an Islamic State, and it is extremely important to all Kuwaitis that their children are exposed to the teachings of Islam in a direct, organized, and meaningful way. All State-operated schools include religion in their basic curriculum,[68] but the need for additional opportunities for those not enrolled in State schools or for those desiring an expanded knowledge of Islamic *Sharia*, has prompted the Kuwaiti government to establish four schools specifically for religious training. In 1989 nearly 5,000 male and female students attended these schools.

As for "special" education, this area has always been a high priority for Kuwaitis. The government has established thirty specialized schools devoted to providing learning opportunities for children with handicaps or other learning disabilities. All of these schools

---

[68] Religion and Arabic are required courses in private schools. All students must take Arabic and all Muslims must take religious courses.

concentrate on helping the students develop skills in practical crafts which will eventually enable them to work and function effectively within the Kuwaiti society.

The Kuwaiti government is constantly looking to the future trying to anticipate the educational needs of the country. As a result of this proactive attitude, one of the educational improvements that has been implemented during recent years is an ambitious undertaking by the Higher Council for Technical and Professional Education in the area of providing training to better prepare Kuwaitis for employment in the coming years.

Perhaps the biggest single problem facing future generations of Kuwaitis will be the make-up of the work force. In past years whenever work was to be done, Kuwait would simply hire immigrants to accomplish the various tasks. The attitude has always been, "Kuwaitis do not do any manual labor." Contributing to this rapidly worsening problem has been the government's heavy emphasis on the desirability of obtaining a higher education and mastering the professions combined with traditional Kuwaiti mind sets, such as, "Why should I do the work, when I can pay someone else to do it?" or, "I don't do the work, I manage it."

Kuwait is seriously lagging behind many countries in the world in applied technical or vocational training, which can be described as focused training to prepare an individual to assume a specific and important type of occupation that usually requires working with the hands, as well as the mind. The Kuwaiti social structure has a negative attitude toward manual labor of any kind and toward vocational and non-managerial work in particular. It did not take long for us to observe this attitude when we were in Kuwait. In fact, none of us can remember ever seeing a Kuwaiti doing manual labor. Some of the Kuwaiti men we have met are more than capable of performing these important labor-intensive type tasks (auto-mechanic, carpenter, cement finisher, painter), and many seem to thoroughly enjoy doing them, but they are performed at home and in the neighborhood, and the Kuwaitis call them "hobbies." The same "work-around-the-house" men would never consider doing the same manual labor as a means of earning income to support their families.

On the positive side, we have not observed that those immigrants who have come to Kuwait to fill these critical jobs are treated as second-class people. Kuwaitis on the whole, appreciate the contribution the immigrant workers make to their society and encomic growth, and they certainly appreciate the fact that the immigrants are relieving them of the need to do the manual work themselves.

Long before the exodus of the immigrant work force from Kuwait resulting from the Iraqi invasion, the Kuwaiti government had recognized that this social attitude problem regarding manual labor was, and would continue to be, a serious problem. In response, a massive campaign was launched in 1985 to attempt to change the prevailing attitude toward vocational and technical training and employment. An article included in the five-year plan that ended in 1990 stated, "The prevalent social outlook towards technical and manual work is a major obstacle to the development of vocational and applied education and professional training. This calls for an intensive effort to bring about a change in attitude and to raise the status of these endeavors in the social values of this society . . . ."

The government's attention to this critical deficiency has begun to show results, as nearly 8,000 Kuwaiti students are currently attending the thirteen different technical colleges and training center, preparing for a variety of technical or vocational jobs, including, but not limited to, accountants, secretaries, nurses, medical technicians, teachers, electricians, and mechanics. It is expected that participation in these colleges will increase substantially as Kuwaitis are forced to adjust to living their lives without the historically present huge immigrant work force.

The effects of the changing work force have already begun to show up in the average Kuwaiti's household. Husbands, wives, and children are now having to do jobs around the house that had typically been the responsibility of the household help, the gardener, the cook, or the driver. Families who once had two or three live-in domestic employees suddenly have one, or even none. Many have found, after the initial shock of having to do things they had never done before, that they are getting along just fine. In fact, some Kuwaitis have indicated they may not rehire all their domestic help, even when workers become more readily available.

Clearly, much remains to be accomplished in regard to Kuwait's evolving educational system. The Kuwaiti government's commitment to educating its people is truly admirable, demonstrating both foresight and dedication to the long-term growth and prosperity of the country. A country's top priority should always be education, and from my discussions with hundreds of Kuwaiti people, it is obvious they are grateful that this fact has been recognized and strongly emphasized by their leadership.

9

BALANCING THE ECONOMY

What They Gonna Do When the Wells Run Dry?

Lee R. Lambert

"The ratification of wealth is not found in mere possession or in lavish expenditure, but in its wise application."

Miquel de Cervantes

The economic structure of Kuwait represents, in one regard, every American's most outrageous, unrealistic dream - - a world with no taxes. No income taxes. No property taxes. Absolutely no taxes!

As a result of the State of Kuwait's outright ownership of all below-ground mineral rights in the country and the State's collection of all associated revenue, there is no need to pass on the cost of operating and maintaining the broad and comprehensive range of the finest government support and services to the residents of Kuwait. In most cases, this wide range of benefits is provided for foreigners and Kuwaiti citizens alike, despite the fact Kuwait's citizens consistently place near the top in the world's annual per capita income statistics ($15,308 in 1989).[69]

---

[69] Kuwait is among the five Arab countries that truly can be categorized as super-rich. The other four are Saudi Arabia, Qatar, United Arab Emirates and Libya. Other Arab nations, including Egypt, Algeria, Oman and Bahrain have small reserves and proportionately small incomes. Iraq, although it has huge oil reserves, is not included in the super-rich due to the tremendous drain on its revenues by the Iran-Iraq war and the Gulf War that followed its August, 1990 invasion of Kuwait.

Kuwait's ability to accomplish this incredible economic feat can be easily explained - - oil! The presence of huge quantities of oil and the bargaining strength of OPEC[70] member countries, combined with the government's aggressive and efficient exploration, production, and distribution system, provides the economic stability that enables this no-tax environment to be successful.

Anyone who has recently visited America's oil producing region in Oklahoma and Texas might have a hard time believing that Kuwait's economy, one of the strongest in the Middle East, could possibly be founded on oil and oil-related products. In America's southwestern states the presence of black gold is obvious. The ubiquitous well heads, with their easily-recognized storage tank assemblies, dot the landscape. American oil wells can be seen in the most unlikely places - - in the back yards of personal residences, on school playgrounds, amidst the pristine beauty of a wheat field ready for harvest, and even in the middle of a grocery store's asphalt parking lot. As if the active wells weren't unsightly enough, America's southwestern landscape is littered with the rusted skeletons of well pumps abandoned once production ceased.

In contrast, the short drive into Kuwait City from the International Airport fails to reveal a single unsightly indicator that one has arrived in the country with the world's third-largest known oil reserves. There simply is no visible evidence of Kuwait's massive oil production industry, which, at its full capacity, can

---

[70] The Organization of Petroleum Exporting Countries (OPEC) was founded in 1960 and comprises thirteen nations. Kuwait is one of seven Arab nation members (Iraq, Algeria, Libya, Qatar, Saudi Arabia and the United Arab Emirates are the others) joining Venezuela, Nigeria, Indonesia, Gabon, Ecuador and Iran.

extract 2.5 million barrels of crude each day.

Most of Kuwait's oil is produced in four main fields, all located well outside Kuwait City. These fields - - Burgan (considered the largest producing field in the world), Magwa, Rawdatain, and Minagish - - are all connected by an intricate system of pipelines, with all the crude oil funneled to a huge, sophisticated tank farm located at Kuwait's oil industry control center outside Ahmadi City.

In comparison with the oil produced in the United States, almost all of which is consumed in the United States, less than ten percent of the oil produced in Kuwait is actually consumed there. The remaining ninety percent is piped through simple gravity fed lines to the export terminal at Mina (port) Ahmadi for shipment to other ports throughout the world. Recently, a sea-island facility located approximately nine miles off shore was completed to accommodate the huge, modern oil-transport tankers. This sea-island complex was the same facility the Coalition forces reluctantly bombed during the Gulf War in order to disable the pumps and prevent continued pollution of the Arabian Gulf waters. Damage from the bombing was extensive; however, repair work progressed well and the facility began operating in early 1992.

I will come back to the economics of oil later, but for now consider the foresight and planning that the leadership of Kuwait has provided in anticipating the need for a long-term strategy for achieving economic diversification and stability. For a country that has nearly 100 billion barrels of producible oil still in the ground, enough of nearly two centuries of sustained production, the decision to selectively invest its oil revenues in areas that would ultimately reduce its dependence on oil and result in a more balanced economic base may seem premature to some other oil rich nations. However, Kuwait's ability to continue to function financially as a nation in exile, despite the fact the Iraqi invasion completely eliminated revenue from oil production, illustrates the value of the Kuwaiti government's decision to carefully invest for just such a crisis.

Fortunately for its citizens, Kuwait is not like other oil rich countries, who often spend their oil-generated income as fast as it becomes available. Some country's leaders even spend their oil money before it is received through the "creative" use of credit and financing. In contrast, the Al-Sabah-led government anticipated the need many years ago to prepare for their people's economic future. As early as 1976, the issue of what lies ahead for Kuwait was an important one - - so important, in fact, that two trend-setting laws were put into effect in Kuwait. The first was the Social Security Law, which provides for the care of Kuwait's less fortunate citizens, as well as its older generation (The Social Security system is discussed at length in Chapter 6). The second law, assuring the present generation that their grandchildren will be well provided for, is the Future Generations Reserve Law.

Basically, the Future Generations Reserve Law requires the State of Kuwait to set aside ten percent of its total annual revenues for future generations. In a classically shrewd Kuwaiti financial move, the decision was made to ignore the safe "put it in the bank" approach and rather carefully invest the large sums of money accumulating in the Future Generations Fund. The income generated for Kuwait from these Future Generation Fund investments, along with other investment income realized from Kuwait holdings, accounts for more than half the total gross revenue generated in

Kuwait including all oil production related income. Kuwait's foreign investment portfolio is said to be in the range of $100 billion,[71] with nearly seventy percent of the total amount earmarked for this innovative Future Generations Fund. Estimates place the daily income from this extensive Kuwaiti investment portfolio at $20 million.

The Kuwaiti government and individual Kuwaiti investors alike prefer to keep a low financial profile.[72] The less publicity their investment activities receive, the better they like it. A number of the world's most deluxe hotels, seaside resorts, and world-class ski resorts are owned either outright by the Kuwaiti government or groups of Kuwaiti investors, but the Kuwaiti involvement is typically unknown to the general public. For example, Kuwait is the sole owner of the $185 million Atlanta Hilton and is the major shareholder in the famous Phoenician Resort Hotel in Scottsdale, Arizona. (This deluxe property was once managed by Charles Keating, who has been convicted of fraud in connection with his savings & loan dealings.)[73] In Canada, the Blackcomb Ski and Vacation Resort, located on Whistler Mountain, an hour's drive

---

[71] As a result of the Iraqi invasion and subsequent Gulf War, Kuwait's investment portfolio has been significantly reduced (estimates range from 50 to 70 percent) in order to repay the costs incurred by the Coalition countries and to expedite the Kuwait rebuilding process until the revenue-producing oil industry has recovered.

[72] Although they have received a great deal of publicity, the Kuwaitis are far down the list of leading investors in the United States. To the surprise of many, top U.S. investors are the Dutch with over $9 billion in holdings, Great Britain, Canada and Germany are next in order and account for a total of nearly $20 billion.

[73] Kuwait had no connection with Charles Keating beyond the significant financial investment in the Arizona resort property. Kuwait was never associated in any way with Mr. Keating's fraud complaints or eventual convictions.

from Vancouver, British Columbia, benefited from heavy Kuwaiti financial participation.

In 1973, Kuwait purchased Kiawah Island in South Carolina with the intention of turning it into an idyllic beach resort. After investing $200 million, Kuwaiti investors became disappointed with the slow development process and sold the island in 1988, barely recouping the original investment.

The list of unpublicized Kuwaiti investments is, no doubt, extensive, but the State of Kuwait holdings that have been made public reveal that the financial brain trust for this tiny nation, who conduct business as the Kuwait Investment Office from the St. Vedast House in London, are also extremely successful in selecting and managing an extremely profitable mix of investments.

Some of Kuwait's largest holdings are in Europe, where the ten percent stake in British Petroleum translates to an investment of over $3.5 billion. Kuwait has also poured another $3 billion into acquiring fourteen percent ownership in Daimler-Bentz of Germany. America's Santa Fe International, an oil exploration company, is wholly owned by Kuwait and is currently valued at over $2.5 billion. Hoechst, the giant German chemical company, has benefited from over $2 billion of Kuwaiti capital, giving the men at St. Vedast House a twenty-three percent ownership in that corporation.

Further evidence of Kuwait's international investments and economic diversification is borne out by the fact that Kuwait maintains substantial positions in most of the New York Stock Exchange's leading 100 corporations. This heavy investment in the U.S. stock market includes more than three million shares of International Business Machine. Kuwait's IBM stock portfolio is valued at approximately $300 million.

The well-managed, balanced Kuwaiti investment portfolio gives the government the ability to continue functioning effectively despite difficulties that
may arise in the oil industry. In fact, thanks to the
foresight of those who developed and implemented the
Kuwaiti economic strategy, the 1990 Iraqi invasion and
nearly seven-month occupation of Kuwait, including
Saddam Hussein's attempt to destroy Kuwait's oil production capability, failed to have the crippling effect on
Kuwait that was anticipated by uninformed financial
analysts around the world. The Kuwaiti government
continued to function efficiently in exile in Saudi
Arabia. Students and families outside of Kuwait received regular and supplemental support payments in
a timely manner, while the other financial dealings of
the State, including large payments toward the cost of
the Gulf War, were accomplished by liquidating portions of the huge Kuwaiti investment portfolio.

The Iraqi invasion and the turmoil that followed
is not the first significant economic challenge Kuwait
has managed to overcome. In the past twenty years
worldwide oil conservation, for example, has resulted
in the reduction of Kuwait's oil production from a high
in 1972 of 3.3 million barrels a day to a pre-invasion
figure that hovered around one million barrels a day.
The result: a 66 percent drop in oil-related revenue.
Tighter fiscal control and the expansion of non-oil-
related revenue producing efforts, such as international
investments and small private industrial endeavors,
has helped Kuwait overcome this difficult situation.

A major financial crisis occurred in 1982 when
Kuwait's secondary "unofficial" stock market, (Souk Al-
Manakh),[74] which was established by greedy specula-

---

[74] Literally translated means "resting place for camels."

tors and initially operated from a parking garage, collapsed, leaving some 6,000 investors holding unhonored, post-dated checks (futures) valued at KD 27 billion or $92 billion. The net effect of the crash of the Souk Al-Manakh was far more devastating than the losses incurred by the 6,000 participating investors. The official Kuwait Stock Market was heavily impacted as well, and in 1983 trading volume decreased 57 percent from the previous year. The Kuwaiti government had to intervene and develop a method to allow devastated investors to recover as much of their money as possible, while instituting policies that would prevent a similar disaster from recurring. The country's financial community is still struggling to fully recover from this 1982 stock market crisis. Nearly every financially oriented conversation in which I have been involved eventually gets around to discussing the Souk Al-Manakh.

Even before invading Kuwait, Iraq played a role in undermining Kuwait's economic stability through its escalation of the Iran-Iraq war, which raged violently in the region for almost eight years before its 1988 conclusion. The effect that conflict had on Kuwait's huge entrepot[75] trade business was profoundly negative as commercial shippers abandoned most Middle East ports near the Iran-Iraq war zone. Once again the Kuwaiti government acted quickly to overcome this problem, encouraging shippers to return by eliminating nearly all re-export restrictions and encouraging rapid expansion of Kuwaiti private industrial development to replace the lost entrepot trade.

Now let's return to the economics of oil. Al-

---

[75] Entrepot is defined by the *American Heritage Dictionary* as; "A place where goods are stored or deposited and from which they are distributed; A trading or market center."

though Great Britain and America played a significant role in enabling Kuwait to develop the exploitation of its oil to finance a variety of modernization projects, the three-way partnership ended in 1980 when both foreign partners were bought out and the Kuwait Petroleum Corporation (KPC) was established. Extensive road networks, modern communication systems, the region's best schools, the latest medical facilities and equipment, and the most current housing styles are constant reminders of those big-money, oil-boom days of the 1970s and early 1980s.

Shifting with the times, Kuwait has begun to refocus its oil industry toward achieving much less dependency on the sale of crude oil products and aggressively expanding its capability to produce and market refined petroleum products. A case in point: KPC now owns over 5,000 retail gasoline service stations in several European countries. Some of the stations (I happened to notice two while driving through the English countryside around London) carry the unique and ingeniously appropriate name of "Q8."

The processing or refining of crude oil into finished products, as well as the transportation of these products and crude oil to world markets has been developed to near perfection by the Kuwaiti oil sector. The three Kuwaiti oil refineries have a total processing capacity of over 600,000 barrels per day. The most modern of these refineries is Shuaiba, which began operation in 1968. The Shuaiba Refinery is completely powered by hydrogen and utilizes an extremely complex control system to switch from heavy petroleum to medium or light products at the mere push of a button. This operational flexibility allows Shuaiba to handle more than thirty different types of products, depending upon market demand.

The Kuwait Oil Tanker Company, which was also acquired by KPC in 1980, is considered one of the world's most efficient and modern oil tanker companies. The company is constantly investigating ways to improve capacity and reduce or optimize manpower, subsequently increasing profit margins. The firm's fleet of over fifty tankers of various sizes and functions continues to maintain one of the industries highest performance efficiency records, despite a severely depressed petroleum shipping market.

A tightly managed oil industry and very successful involvement in the foreign investment arena still have not satisfied the Kuwait government's desire for long-term security through a more balanced, diversified economic strategy. The government realizes that if Kuwait is ever to attain its desired degree of self-reliance, it will be absolutely necessary to establish and nurture the country's non-oil industrial sector.

This may prove to be a difficult assignment. As recently as 1983, the crucial industrial segment of the Kuwaiti economy was able to generate no more than four percent of the gross national product (GNP). Since then, the situation has improved slightly. Of Kuwait's 1989s $30 billion GNP, a relatively small, but substantially improved, 17 percent ($5 billion) was contributed by the Kuwaiti industrial sector. There are fears, however, that this 17 percent contribution may be nearing a maximum level, given the problems facing this Kuwaiti industrial sector.

This industrial area has always contended with the difficulties of a severe lack of raw materials. Now, following the physical devastation that accompanied the Iraqi invasion, they must also deal with a serious shortage of appropriately skilled manpower, which resulted from a huge exodus of foreigners during the Iraqi occupation. In addition to the loss of skilled labor, this exodus of foreign workers and their families has had another severe impact - - the shrinking of an already small local market (pre-invasion population was almost 2.2 million while the post-invasion population is expected to hover around 1.5 million for several years). The challenges facing Kuwait in this area are daunting, even discouraging.

Recognizing the importance of this economic sector, however, the Kuwaiti government has continued to attempt to shape their future by establishing specifically designated industrial zones with new, modern warehousing, business, and small manufacturing facilities provided to encourage new enterprise. Additionally, in much the same way as the American Small Business Administration supports growth in this area, Kuwait has established organizational and consultative institutions to assist in the research, development and implementation of industrial sector projects. For nearly ten years, I have undertaken management consulting and training assignments for two organizations that serve the Kuwaiti industrial sector in an advisory capacity: The Kuwait Foundation for the Advancement of Sciences (KFAS) and the Kuwait Institute of Scientific Research (KISR).

KFAS, which can be compared to America's Ford Foundation or the National Science Foundation, was the first organization of its kind in the Arab world. This important organization receives the bulk of its support from private Kuwaiti shareholding companies, who contribute five percent of their annual net profit to the KFAS Fund. Although KFAS is a non-profit, non-governmental institution, it was originally suggested and founded in 1976 by the current Amir, who was Crown Prince at the time, His Highness Sheikh Jabar Al-

Ahmed Al-Jaber Al-Sabah. The Amir serves as the Chairman of the Board for KFAS. The general goals of KFAS are to support activities targeted at modernization and scientific development within the State of Kuwait. The annual operating budget for KFAS is typically in the range of $8-10 million.

Kuwaiti citizens and non-Kuwaitis with a Kuwaiti co-sponsor or organizations that feel they have a viable idea that will spawn a new industry, improve existing business conditions, or enhance the environment in Kuwait or elsewhere in the region, can propose a research project to KFAS for funding. A review committee specializing in the area of the proposal will make evaluations and funding recommendations after each proposal is judged on its technical merit and eventual benefit to Kuwait or the region. Obviously, those projects with technological application providing a high potential for return on investments are given first priority. The KFAS projects dealing specifically with applied science - - aquaculture and agriculture and animal production - - are vital to the Kuwaiti's long-term economic future. These types of projects focus on identifying and developing model enterprises, suitable for the difficult Kuwait climate conditions, which can eventually be converted into commercially viable endeavors for the critical food-related industries.

KFAS recognizes and awards monetary prizes for significant scientific accomplishments by members of the Arab world at the annual Kuwait Prize ceremony. It also conducts local and overseas professional training seminars and symposia; authors, translates and publishes significant scientific publications; and develops and disseminates culture-related scientific material (evaluating scientific findings in the context of Islamic culture), as well as sponsoring a variety of scientific activities including competitions such as the International Mathematics, Chemistry and Physics Olympiad.

On two separate occasions, in 1986 and in 1990, we were fortunate enough to be present in Kuwait for the festivities associated with the Kuwait Prize. We all agree that it was an experience we will never forget. The event is to the Arabic community what the Pulitzer Prize is to the rest of the world. This gala affair is truly a "media event" and usually brings out the elite of the Arab scientific sector as well as a long list of other Arab dignitaries to watch as awards are made for outstanding achievement in five distinct categories: basic science, applied science, arts and letters, Arabic and Islamic culture, and economic and social sciences. Recognition is given to Kuwaitis and citizens of other Arab countries in each category, Monetarily speaking, the Kuwait Prize is not as substantial as the Pulitzer, but KD10,000 ($35,000) is a sum not to be ignored.[76] Based on my years of providing management consulting services to some of the world's most dedicated research and development scientists, I have concluded that money, unless it is targeted for additional research opportunities, is usually of secondary concern. To the true scientist, it is the recognition by their peers that is the real prize.

Attending one of the Kuwait Prize ceremonies is an opportunity. Being included in the audience at two of these prestigious programs is an honor, indeed. The bad news, however, is that the entire two hour program is conducted in Arabic. The first time we were invited, we learned to watch the crowd and the presenter closely - - when they laughed, we laughed, and when they applauded, we applauded. Our host, Dr. Abbas

---

[76] In special circumstances the Kuwait Prize can be as much as $100,000.

Alikhan, sensed our discomfort and attempted to interpret as much as possible, but it was still a long evening. However, by the time we found ourselves at the 1990 affair, my daughter, Erin, had three years of classic Arabic instruction behind her, and remarkably, she was able to translate most of the important comments; and the evening passed more quickly.

Because of the importance of the Kuwait Prize, the award ceremony is taped for local television broadcast several times in the days following the event. Attired in Western suits and dresses, it is obvious we are not one of the Arab contingent; therefore, we consistently receive considerable air time as the inquisitive cameramen frequently pan their cameras to our section of the audience between awards. In fact, over the past few years, we have probably been seen on Kuwaiti television more than the frequently absent Johnny Carson was seen on America's NBC Network.

Additionally, each time I conduct a management seminar or give a speech for the Engineering Society or Kuwait University, the video cameras are rolling. We constantly get calls at our hotel from local friends who learn of our visit through a television show and wish to welcome us back to Kuwait. Thanks to Kuwaiti television and its in-depth coverage of local events, a Lambert family visit to Kuwait is never a secret. It is fun to be thought of as "celebrities," even though we realize it is usually because there is not much else happening; or as we would say in America, our Kuwaiti television appearances come on "slow news days."

The Kuwait Institute for Scientific Research (KISR) is the other major institution dedicated to investigating and developing concepts and techniques which will have a positive impact on the future economic and social growth of Kuwait. The concept for KISR dates back to 1967, but KISR did not become a fully functioning research institute until 1973. Originally established with Japanese participation through the Arab Oil Company Ltd., KISR is organized and managed by technical specialty area, very much like Battelle Memorial Institute, one of our country's premier research groups and the largest contract research organization in the world. It was during my nearly ten years of teaching research project management at Battelle that I first became acquainted with the people of Kuwait. KISR, which frequently conducts KFAS funded projects, focuses much of the attention of its 1,000 staff scientists and support professionals in the areas of food resources, marine biology, fisheries, archeology, the petrochemical industry, and economics. Prior to the Iraqi invasion, the KISR operating budget was more than KD20 million ($68 million). Initially, almost all of the KISR funding was taken from the government budget (unlike KFAS, KISR is a government-funded agency). However, in recent years, Kuwait's constrained economy and the government's desire to promote cooperation between government and private industry has encouraged the KISR management to secure approximately 25 percent of its funding from non-governmental sources.

Unfortunately, what was once the best equipped and most professionally staffed research and development facility in the Arab world is now a looted, burned out shell. All the expensive, sophisticated equipment and critical research reference materials housed in the National Center for Science and Technology, along with critical research results and records, were removed or destroyed by Iraqi invaders. No one is willing to estimate how much it will cost or how long it will take to rebuild KISR to its former glory, but I am sure the rebuilding process will be measured in millions of dollars and years of effort.

One of KISR's highest priority research areas is in developing and improving Kuwait's food production and processing capabilities to help reduce the almost total dependence upon availability of food from imports. Believe it or not, despite the focus on oil, harsh weather conditions, and a severe lack of adequate irrigation water for the marginally fertile soil, Kuwait has managed to develop an agriculture sector that yields enough of certain types of vegetable crops to meaningfully supplement the imported crops necessary to meet the needs of its small population. I was shocked to learn that Kuwait's agricultural efforts have been so successful in growing greenhouse tomatoes that tomatoes have become Kuwait's primary crop, exceeding local needs and eliminating the need to import. Other crops that thrive in the current Kuwait environment are strawberries, cauliflower, lettuce, eggplant, and onions. Kuwait is attempting to expand its present 20 million square meters of cultivated, crop producing land, but today the Kuwaiti agricultural crop production still satisfies only a very small percentage of the country's needs.

In recent visits to Kuwait, I have seen evidence of the growth of a small, but flourishing, animal husbandry sector of the overall economic structure. Heavy investments by the Kuwaiti government, independent agriculture interests, and local livestock companies have begun to yield results. In the past few years hundreds of Frisian cows (a rugged breed that is able to survive extreme environmental conditions) have been imported into Kuwait from Holland and Denmark. At the same time, millions of chickens were purchased from Lebanon, India, and various European locations. Finally, Turkey, Australia, and European countries sold Kuwait large flocks of sheep and goats. The Kuwaitis have nurtured these animals and continue to strengthen the breeding process to improve their tolerance for the severe Kuwaiti desert and weather conditions.

By far the most successful of the Kuwaiti efforts to decrease its dependence on foreign suppliers of meat, milk, and eggs has been in the area of poultry. Currently, Kuwait's poultry business provides nearly 50 percent of the chicken meat required in the country while also accounting for over 50 percent of the eggs purchased by Kuwaiti consumers. The production rates are continually increasing, as 200 million eggs and 20,000 tons of meat were produced in each of the past few years.

The local contribution to Kuwait's total need in mutton and beef is significantly less, but the latest estimates reveal locally raised sheep account for almost fifteen percent of the country's needs, while beef is a distant third, at just over seven percent of the total consumed quantity coming from the local sources. Some thirty dairy farms produce over 30,000 tons of fresh milk each year, which accounts for over twenty-five percent of the total Kuwaiti need.

A very active commercial fishing industry has evolved, and one of the highlights of all our trips to Kuwait is arriving at the public fish market on Gulf Street around 3 p.m. when the fishermen bring in their day's catch. This incredibly busy market is not a tourist attraction. It is an active market where the locals come to select their fresh catch of the day for the evening meal.

The first time we visited the Kuwaiti fish market my wife, Carolyn, and my daughter, Erin, were very reluctant to go in. They looked through the big double doors and saw hundreds of people trudging through shallow pools of water, slipping on fish slime, as they attempted to avoid the still flipping fish that had managed to work their way off the display tables onto the floor. Clearly, this wasn't America's neighborhood Safeway store. Finally, we found a dry path to a nearby table, and the girls agreed to give it a try.

Our good friend, Adnan Al-Abdulmuhsen was our guide, and it was a real experience to watch him bargain (the Arabs love to bargain on almost anything) with the men behind the counter. He would pick the Hamour (sea bass), Zabedi (Gulf's own breed), or huge shrimp that were to his liking from the thousands of varieties displayed on tables lining all four walls. Once he found the fish that met his strict quality standards, Adnan immediately began trying to convince the vendor behind the table to lower his price. Eventually, sometimes after Adnan walked away to let the vendor consider his offer, the two reached an agreement. The vendor then cleaned the fish for preparation, packaged it and sent us on our way to a great gastronomical treat. The only thing in America that comes close to this fish-buying ritual is the process that takes place between the would-be automobile buyer and the high-pressure used-car salesman. These fish selection and price-bargaining experiences are so entertaining and educational that we have made it a point of recording it on video for our friends in America.

The fish of the Arabian Gulf are extremely good eating, and Kuwaitis will often treat special dinner guests to a sampling of several delicious varieties. Unfortunately, because of heavy fishing activity the past few years, the yield from the once-bountiful sea has dropped dramatically. The governments of the Arabian Gulf region have joined forces to implement controls and restrictions in order to insure that fishing will remain a viable industry and, therefore, a positive contributor to the Kuwaiti economic mix.

Kuwait's economy will always be heavily dependent on imports, as evidenced by the nearly $2 billion spent each year on products, goods, and services from America and Japan. However, the government intends to continue its attempts to reduce this dependency as much as possible. The primary areas of import for the American suppliers are passenger cars, car and tractor replacement parts, heating and air-conditioning equipment, and tobacco products.

Although the number of organizations and the specific type of American presence in Kuwait may be altered as a result of the "post-invasion" conditions, many of the same companies are expected to surface including: American Express, Arthur Young & Company, Avis, Bausch & Lomb, Boeing, Crown Pacific, Ernest & Whinny, Hardee's Food Systems, IBM, Lockheed, McDonnell-Douglas, Merrill Lynch, NCR, Otis Elivator, Pepsi-Cola, Pratt & Whitney, Raytheon, Rockwell International, and Sheraton Hotels.

The Kuwait economy generates and spends considerable money. Therefore, banking has become big business in Kuwait, especially in the past ten years. In accordance with normal Kuwaiti practice, the best financial information, banking equipment, processes, and management philosophy have been gleaned from leading banks throughout the world and then carefully tailored to the emirate's specific banking environment. Unfortunately, the Kuwait banking community has experienced some difficulty during recent years. Uncontrolled expansion, poor loan selection and management, falling world oil consumption with the associated depressed prices, and the lingering effects of the Souk Al-Manakh collapse have all contributed to a serious strain on the banking sector.

I have been told by some reliable Kuwaiti sources that the Kuwaiti economic planners at the Central Bank of Kuwait, which controls the country's banking system and monetary policy, are considering the benefits of a major overhaul of the banking sector on the heals of the Iraqi invasion. Potentially, pressure will be exerted to consolidate smaller Kuwaiti banks into three or four strong, well capitalized institutions. A move in this direction will be consistent with the current trend in America and the rest of the financial world, which is attempting to gain the advantages of merging banks to create a much larger financial base while reducing or eliminating many operational overhead costs.

The official currency of the State of Kuwait is the Kuwait Dinar. Prior to the Iraqi invasion in August of 1990, the Kuwait Dinar was among the strongest currency in the world. At the time of the Iraqi invasion, one KD was worth approximately US $3.40. Kuwait issued its first currency in April, 1961, after one failed attempt was recorded in 1950. The new official Kuwait currency replaced the Indian Rupee, which had been a familiar currency in circulation throughout the Arabian Gulf region for many years. The Kuwait Dinar is equal to 10 Dirhams or 1,000 Fils. These same denominations continue in effect today as Kuwait has a complete range of coins and paper notes in distribution. Following the Iraqi occupation and looting of all the banks in Kuwait, the government canceled all currency previously in circulation and issued newly minted paper notes. New coins were not minted.

Perhaps the smallest contributors to the Kuwaiti economic picture, but the most noticeable and enjoyable for many foreign visitors, are the never-ending rows of *souks* (markets) selling every imaginable type of product. A day wandering through these small shops in any of Kuwait's numerous shopping districts (see Chapter 3) is truly an experience not to be missed. Shoppers can find anything and everything if they have the patience to continue to search until they locate the *souk* that deals in their desired product. Most of the *souks* would be what we, in America, consider specialty shops selling a broad range of brand names, but in a very specific category. There is even a "Friday market" which sells new and second-hand items of every imaginable kind in the American garage-sale or yard-sale tradition, as customers visit the huge vacant lot filled with previously owned merchandise.

While Kuwait is clearly a free-enterprise oriented economy, it remains necessary for the Kuwaiti government to continue as the country's main source of economic activity and stability, as well as the principal stimulator behind economic reform and expansion.

Potentially, the far reaching impact of the Iraqi invasion on the Kuwaiti economy could be very negative. However, it is possible that the substantial reduction in population and the shift in labor-force utilization may ultimately drive Kuwait to more expediently implement important modifications in its economic policies with the net effect being a stronger and more self-reliant economy.

Regardless of what takes place in the next few years, it must be comforting to the Kuwaiti people to know that their government is not waiting to see what happens when the oil runs out. Instead, the Kuwaiti government aggressively continues to seek ways of improving the country's economic condition through a diversified and balanced Kuwait economic policy.

10

ENTERTAINMENT AND RECREATION

Kuwaitis Get High On Life

Erin Lambert

"Laughter is the sun that drives winter from the human face."
Victor Hugo

Alcoholic beverages of all kinds are illegal in Kuwait, and so, unlike the Western world, where alcohol seems to be the centerpiece of most social occasions, Kuwaitis must find other means of entertainment. In the middle of the desert this is not always easy to do! The Kuwaitis do seem to manage, though; in fact, they spend about four or five hours each day eating, talking, and just being social. Evenings are filled with laughter, food , family, and friends; weekends typically center around family fun in amusement parks, beach resorts, and desert camp grounds. Despite what Americans might consider limited resources, Kuwaitis always seem to have plenty of fun to fill their days.

The preferred method of entertaining guests in Kuwait involves elaborate, lavishly prepared lunch and dinner parties at home. The Kuwaitis feel strongly about inviting friends and relatives, as well as out-of-town guests, to their homes to share in the comfort and warmth of their sincere hospitality. On many occasions my family has been invited to dine in Kuwaiti homes, where husbands, wives, and children and household help have worked diligently all day to prepare a

"Thanksgiving-like" feast. Usually the large dining room table is literally filled to capacity with appetizers, main courses, fruits, juices, and desserts. In America these "Kuwaiti-style" feasts are usually reserved for special holidays, with the balance of the social entertaining being achieved in restaurants or clubs, but in Kuwait such events occur at any time.

Two of the most popular and delicious appetizers are *hummous* and *tabbouleh. Hummous*, originally a Syrian dish, is a mixture of dried chick peas, *tahini* (a thick paste made from toasted sesame seeds), lemon juice, garlic, salt, and paprika. The ingredients are mixed until they form a thick, smooth puree which is served in a hollow dish with a small amount of olive oil in the center. *Tabbouleh*, originally from Syria or Lebanon, is a salad made of chopped parsley, chopped fresh mint, *burghul* (whole wheat which has been dried in the sun and then crushed), chopped spring onions, chopped garlic, chopped tomatoes, lemon, salt, black pepper, oil, and a few crisp lettuce leaves. A bowl is lined with the lettuce leaves and the salad is placed on top. Other typical Kuwaiti appetizers are *falafel* (deep-fried bean croquettes), *kibbeh mishwi* (stuffed ground meat balls), *warak al inab* (stuffed grape leaves), and *samboosa* (pastries filled with vegetables, meat, or cheese).

After the appetizers, of course, comes the main course, consisting of chicken, fish, and lamb or beef -- pork is never served because of the strict Islamic dietary restrictions. Fish is more popular in the Middle East than in the United States, and there are almost as many methods of preparing fish as there are varieties of fish from Gulf waters. The most common fish are *hamour*, which is similar to what Americans refer to as sea bass, king-sized prawns, and the *zabedi*, which is a white fish species unique to the Gulf. Fish dishes are served with rice, and depending on the type of fish, each dish of rice is flavored with a different spice. If fish is not your favorite, don't worry; there is always chicken - - stewed, roasted, grilled or barbecued, marinated in lemon juice and spices, or stuffed with savory rice, fruits, and nuts. Meat (beef and lamb) is also a popular Kuwaiti main course and is served ground, mashed, stuffed, cubed or kebabed. Rice, the staple of food in the Gulf, is served with every meal - - garnished with almonds and raisins, sweetened with honey and rosewater, delicately tinted with saffron threads, steeped in tasty meat stock and spices, or cooked together with onions or lentils.

One needs an extremely sweet tooth to eat Kuwaiti desserts, which are traditionally flavored with cardamon, saffron and rosewater. Almonds, pistachios, cashews, raisins, yogurt, and cheese are also common ingredients. *Muhallabiya* (milk pudding) is popular in Kuwait, and most pastries are deep fried, then saturated in Shirra, a sweet syrup made from lemon juice, rosewater, and sugar.

I will always remember my first meal in a Kuwaiti home. Dr. Abbas, my father's associate from the Kuwait Foundation for the Advancement of Sciences, had invited our family, as well as a few of his close friends, to his home for a traditional Kuwaiti meal. I must admit I was a bit nervous. Would they expect me to sit on the floor? Would I have to eat with my hands? What would happen if I did not like something? Fortunately, I did not have to deal with any of these concerns because there were chairs and silverware, and the food was delicious!

As my family walked up to Dr. Abbas' front door, we noticed that the front patio was lined with a pen full of chickens and pheasants on one side and nearly twenty pairs of shoes on the other. We rang the doorbell, and Dr. Abbas greeted us with a big smile, indicating that we should remove our shoes before entering. In the United States removing one's shoes is considered strange, even rude, but in Kuwait removing one's shoes before entering the house is normal in respect for Islamic cleanliness standards as well as avoiding tracking the dust and fine Kuwait sand into the house.

Dr. Abbas ushered us into his family room, where we witnessed his entire family of seven carrying huge platters of food from the restaurant-style kitchen into the dining room. The dining room table was completely filled with platters and bowls of tempting food. It looked to me like enough to feed an army, so I dug in. We had appetizers, rice, chicken, shrimp, lamb, and American mini-pizzas made especially for us, although we discovered later that pizza is a big favorite in Kuwait. With plates full of food, we gathered in the family room, where we sat around casually on one of the many couches, and enjoyed our meal and began making new friends. For small gatherings or family dinners, the meal is usually served on the dining table. But for large groups the Kuwaitis, just like Americans, usually gather in the family or living room for a more informal and relaxed environment. The only things missing were the TV trays.

Once the meal was over, it was time to have tea and talk - - two of the Kuwaitis favorite pastimes. Dr. Abbas told us stories about the "olden days" in Kuwait and tales about the ten years he spent as a student at Penn State University in the United States, where he earned his Bachelors, Masters and Doctorate Degrees in Petroleum Engineering. We discussed the major differences between the Islam religion and Christianity, and we even experienced a little bit of the Kuwaiti wildlife when Dr. Abbas' son brought in one of his pet birds and decided to put it on my sister Marnie's shoulder. Marnie, who was a sophomore at Miami University of Ohio at the time, had passed up the traditional American college spring break in sunny Florida to join the rest of the family in Kuwait. She was not keen on the idea of a bird perched on her shoulder, but Dr. Abbas' son did not understand her objections, so onto Marnie's shoulder the bird went - - literally. As we quickly tried to clean the "mess" off her shoulder, I looked around the room at the faces of twenty laughing people, both Arabs and Americans, and realized that we were not really very different from each other at all.

You don't have to visit a Kuwaiti's home to enjoy a great meal and engage in some interesting conversations with old friends. Every time our family visits Kuwait it is customary to have at least one meal at the Palm Palace Restaurant in the Salmiya shopping district. The Palm Palace is one of the best known restaurants in Kuwait. Aziz Al-Abdulmuhsen, the brother of our good friend Adnan, is the owner. Because the selection and preparation of Middle Eastern food is outstanding, each time we visit the Palm Palace we are guilty of having eyes much bigger than our stomachs, and leave with plenty of doggie bags filled for snacking in our hotel room. We never have gone to the Palm Palace without meeting several business or social acquaintances, who willingly take the time from their meals to share stories about the latest events in Kuwait.

One of my fondest memories of Kuwait came during one of the late night dinner parties. Nabil Qaddumi, an engineer with degrees from Stanford and MIT, who had joined my dad as a lecturer for a Kuwait training seminar, invited us to his home for dinner. As usual the food was plentiful and delicious, but, the conversation during and after the meal was what I remember best. My brother, Davin, and Nabil have something in common: they are both big Oakland (both of them will refuse to acknowledge the team moved to Los Angeles years ago) Raider football fans. For over two hours the men and the women, who were surprisingly well informed about the sport, argued over which National Football League (NFL), or which college team was the biggest, meanest, and fastest. It was amazing. We could just as well have been in our family room in Worthington, Ohio. Most Kuwaitis don't see live football on their television, but the true football fans in Kuwait all have video tapes of the Saturday and Sunday games in the United States delivered to them the next week so they can keep pace with their favorite team's progress.[77] The evening ended after 2 a.m. with the issue of which football team was the best left to be settled another day.

Although eating is the main source of entertainment in Kuwait, it is certainly not the only one. Kuwaitis, like Americans, have many other hobbies and interests to occupy their time. A popular pastime in Kuwait City is walking for hours along the Arabian Gulf, on a fifteen mile stretch of beautiful brick walkways. Leisure time is also spent in restaurants and parks, or "cruising" the strip in the Salmiya shopping area - - this source of entertainment is normally reserved for the young, teenaged Kuwaiti and immigrant men.

Entertainment City was an exciting way to have

---

[77] Thanks to powerful satellite dishes and the post-Gulf War availability of U.S. Armed Forces Radio, it is much easier for the Kuwaiti sports fans to keep track of their favorite teams.

fun in Kuwait, until the August 2nd Iraqi invasion, when the Iraqi military forces disassembled or destroyed every part of the Disney-like amusement park. It is situated in the middle of the desert near Doha Village, about twelve miles north of Kuwait City, and offered fun for young and old alike. The original construction of this multi-million-dollar amusement park was truly an international effort, with designers from the United States, contractors from Italy, rides and installers from Switzerland, France, and Italy, and thousands of laborers from Asia and the Middle East.

The park was divided into three distinct Worlds - - Arab World, Future World, and International World. Kids once enjoyed rides with names such as Oasis Express, Arab Gulf Ride, American Carousel, Sinbad the Sailor, American Railroad, Atom Smasher, and Australian Log Ride. After the rides parents would buy ice cream at the Space Station restaurant or purchase a delicious hamburger from Kuwait's own version of McDonald's - - The Hungry Bunny. There were plenty of attractions to keep the kids busy at Kuwait's desert mini-Disneyland, especially the young kids, who came from throughout the Gulf to visit Entertainment City. Currently, plans are being implemented for rebuilding Entertainment City to be even better than it was before the Iraqi invasion with portions of the park scheduled to reopen in August 1992.

Weekends and holidays in Kuwait are good times to get away from the hustle and bustle of the big city, and Kuwaitis frequently head for beach resorts or private beach villas along the Gulf coast. Kuwaiti families spend a great deal of time sitting on the beach, relaxing. We had a chance one year to visit Kuwait's newest leisure locations - - Khiran Resort. Our friend Adnan and his family were our hosts at this beautiful spot, located about sixty miles south of Kuwait City and only twelve miles from the Saudi Arabia border. The resort is lovely and all 148 chalets and a modern marina were filled to capacity when we were there. The scene at the beach was a bit unusual for us. Kuwaitis, because of their strict Islamic religious beliefs restricting public exposure of the body, do not wear bathing suits at the beach. Instead they spread blankets on the beach and sit fully clothed in the intense heat drinking tea and talking. Most families take at least one of their household workers on these weekend retreats so that mom and dad can relax and have time to visit as they watch their children romp along the beach, and build sand castles, or fish, as do children everywhere.

Khiran Resort was opened in 1987, but the oldest tourist complex in Kuwait is situated on historical Failaka Island. This attractive complex, just minutes from the shores of Kuwait City by hovercraft, has 472 elegantly furnished chalets available together with restaurants, shops, and a motorized tram that shuttles visitors around the complex.

Team sports are also an obvious form of entertainment in Kuwait, and there are many from which to chose. Cricket seems to be the most popular, with more cricket teams in Kuwait than all other sporting organizations combined. Squash is one of the favorite sports, and most major hotels provide courts for residents and club members. The Hunting and Equestrian Club is home to the Kuwait Archery Center, which hosts several local and regional competitions yearly. Other Kuwaiti sports include motor racing, judo, darts, chess, sailing, wind surfing, badminton, fishing, and believe it or not, ice skating. Kuwait boasts a modern ice skating complex with two rinks and seating for 1,600 people. Because of the intense desert heat, these ice rinks are always very busy. Many Kuwaiti families enjoy ice skating at the local rink, and expert instruction is available for those desiring to take part in competitions such as figure skating or ice hockey.

In addition to some of these rather unusual sports, there are the more typical ones such as rugby, baseball, swimming, and soccer (Kuwaitis know it as football), as the most visible and popular among the younger generation. Along every stretch of road, wherever there is a big enough space in the sand, kids as well as adults (all males) set up goals and enjoy an exciting game of soccer.

Kuwaiti youth, like their American counterparts, lead busy and active lives. Many young girls take dance or music lessons, and most enjoy shopping in the malls for clothing, jewelry, and, of course, music tapes and videos featuring all of the latest popular American and British songs and groups. Almost everywhere I go in Kuwait, I hear the same songs playing on the radio or on my Kuwaiti friend's Walkman that I listen to in Ohio. A majority of the young boys spend their afternoons playing Nintendo or soccer with their friends and generally picking on and harassing their younger siblings. The VCR, and television in general, play a big role in Kuwaiti entertainment. Younger children enjoy the many cartoon videos that are available, and they can even watch a Kuwaiti-produced Arabic Sesame Street, complete with Ernie, Bert and Cookie Monster.

When I first visited Kuwait, I thought I would be bored. I couldn't imagine what the Kuwaitis did to keep busy in their isolated desert homeland. Was I surprised! I have never seen so much activity, so many different things to do and so many places to go. Kuwait has an entertainment or recreation   activity for everyone's taste. Whether you want to simply call on friends and socialize or become involved in sports, or take part in other recreational endeavors such as camping, sailing, and fishing, or almost anything you can dream of - - it is available in Kuwait.

It is obvious to me, Kuwaitis enjoy life. They live it to the fullest while never forgetting to take advantage of every opportunity to share time and experiences with family and friends.

I was relieved to find this friendly Kuwaiti attitude had not changed as a result of the Gulf War. In fact during the first Lambert post-war visit (May-June, 1992) the social activity was at an even more torrid pace than I remembered. Everywhere we went people we knew, and many we had never met, encouraged us to find time for them. Not surprisingly, the Kuwaitis have gained a tremendous new respect - almost admiration - for Americans and they look for ways to demonstrate their feelings. Strangers in elevators invited us to dinner. People in the streets would stop to talk and extend their deepest gratitude for liberating Kuwait. American flags and pictures of President George Bush can be seen throughout Kuwait City. Kuwait will never forget what the American led Coalition accomplished.

We began to understand the sincerity and the depth of this new Kuwaiti-American friendship near the end of our June, 1992 visit. We were being entertained at the home of Salah Al-Mazidi, a Division Director for the Kuwait Institute for Scientific Research (KISR). The Al-Mazidi family had remained in Kuwait for a good portion of the Iraqi occupation and had observed some terrifying and emotional scenes before liberation. To this day, Salah says when President Bush appears on television in Kuwait, his youngest daughter (five years old) will run to the screen and give the American President a big Kuwait "thank you" kiss. As

Americans, we always felt liked in Kuwait, now we feel loved.

11

WAR IN THE GULF

Recovering From the Nightmare

Lee R. Lambert

"I have never advocated war except as a means of peace."

Ulysses S. Grant

On September 28, 1990, His Highness the Amir of the State of Kuwait, Sheikh Jaber Al-Ahmad Al-Jaber Al-Sabah, concluded an historical meeting with the President of the United States, Mr. George Bush. In his farewell remarks on the south lawn of the White House, the Amir thanked the United States for its stand against the Iraqi invasion, "Your principled, courageous and decisive position in the face of the Iraqi aggression on Kuwait is a true expression of the unabated faith and commitment of the American people to the humanitarian morals on which and for which the United States was founded."

The heartsick Kuwaiti Amir made his emotional comments of appreciation only a few days before President Bush addressed the United Nations General Assembly. At that time, he gave the commitment of the United States to oppose the senseless aggression of Iraq perfectly clear. In addressing the General Assembly, President Bush sent a strong message to Iraq, stating emphatically, ". . . the annexation of Kuwait will not be permitted to stand. And this is not simply the view of the United States. It is the view of every Kuwaiti, the

Arab League,[78] The United Nations. Iraq's leaders should listen. It is Iraq against the world." Iraq chose to ignore the warnings. Iraq fought the world and the world won!

Unfortunately, it took almost seven months from the time Iraq launched its brutal pre-dawn attack on an unsuspecting Kuwait for the Iraqi leadership to get the message that it was involved in a battle it could not win. Five and one half months spent attempting to resolve the situation by the most comprehensive diplomatic maneuvering of modern times went unrewarded as the Iraqi leadership clung obstinately to the hope of victory. Against all logic, Iraq ignored U.N. Security Council Resolution 660, which stated: "The U.N. Security Council condemns the Iraqi invasion as a breach of international peace and security, demands the immediate and unconditional withdrawal of Iraqi forces from Kuwait and calls upon Iraq to begin immediate, intensive negotiations."

Finally, with all peaceful means exhausted, a U.N.-sanctioned coalition led by the United States[79] launched a massive military air campaign against Iraq unlike anything the world had ever seen. This incredibly successful forty-day, twenty-four-hour-a-day aerial bombardment, which began the night of January 16, 1991, set the stage for an equally impressive Coalition ground offensive that was almost over before it

---

[78] The Arab League is an organization of 21 Middle Eastern and African nations and the Palestine Liberation Organization, created in 1945. The League's purpose is to promote closer political, economic, cultural, and social relations among the members.

[79] The United States Treasury's reported the cost of the Persian Gulf War to be $61 billion. Kuwait contributed $16 billion and Saudi Arabia added another $16.9 billion. All but $7.3 billion of the total was covered by contributions - - cash and "in-kind" donations - - from U.S. allies in the war.

began on February 23, 1991 (100 hours total duration). The result: Iraq, as promised by the Coalition, suffered an embarrassing defeat and was forced to surrender and withdraw from Kuwait, leaving a great deal of its military arsenal either destroyed, seriously damaged, or in the hands of the coalition forces.

Sadly, in the time it took to enforce the unanimously accepted United Nations Security Council Resolution 660, considerable irreversible damage took place, and the senseless loss of untold thousands of lives was endured by the people of Kuwait and Iraq, as well as other nations throughout the world. In many ways, for Kuwait and the friends of Kuwait, it was truly the worst nightmare imaginable.

Iraq's brutal and naked aggression against Kuwait was, of course, unacceptable to anyone who supports the ideal of freedom and the right of self determination. People around the world, even those who had never heard of Kuwait, were shocked by the viciousness of Saddam Hussein and his minions. By the end of the crisis, as the list of Iraqi atrocities and wanton destruction of property and priceless cultural artifacts grew longer and longer, the entire world was sickened by the actions of the Iraqi aggressors.[80]

Our family's reaction was just as emotional. Obviously, we were hit hard by the events that unfolded in the Arabian Gulf. We had many friends living in Kuwait - - Kuwaitis, Americans, Iraqis, Egyptians, and Palestinians - - and we had no way of knowing whether or not they were safe. August 2 was just like any other morn-

---

[80] The random and wanton destruction levied upon Kuwait by Iraq was terrible. Although obvious evidence of the damage was visible, during my first post-war visit in May of 1992, I was amazed by the reconstruction progress and the general level of recovery that had been achieved in such a short time.

ing for the Lamberts. We turned on our television set to see the latest Cable News Network (CNN) report, and we were shocked to learn of Iraq's overwhelming invasion of Kuwait during the night. The Iraqi invasion had begun at approximately 7 p.m. EDT on August 1, 1990 -- my 44th birthday. Some birthday present!

We had just returned from Atlanta where we celebrated my birthday the night before, telling our friends a variety of Kuwait-related stories, and explaining about our upcoming August trip to London to meet with the officials from the Kuwait Foundation for the Advancement of Sciences (KFAS). We had spent hours in Atlanta answering questions about Kuwait and its people. We explained the American-Kuwaiti high school exchange program that my daughter, Erin, had developed and presented to government officials in Kuwait when she was there the previous May. She was proud to tell our friends that she had just received approval from the administration of our local school district in Worthington, Ohio to conduct a student exchange project in early 1991. Our friends were aware of the recent threats against Kuwait by Iraq and were interested in our opinions about the eventual outcome. Ironically, just hours before Saddam Hussein invaded Kuwait, we had naively assured our friends that Iraq would never resort to military force against a nation of its Arab brothers.

As the Gulf Crises evolved, the irony of significant crisis dates repeated itself. We were just arriving at the parking lot of a local restaurant at 7 p.m., EDT on January 16 when the news on the car radio informed us that the Coalition forces had initiated the air campaign against Iraq. Fully expecting the war to begin at any time after the January 15 United Nations deadline for an Iraqi withdrawal from Kuwait, we reluctantly left the house to celebrate a very special occasion - - Erin's 18th birthday. Some birthday present!

Suddenly no one was interested in eating. We went through the motions, choked on our food, paid the bill, and rushed home to settle in for a long night of CNN telecasts. We managed to squeeze in cake and candles, along with a hurried version of "Happy Birthday", all without taking our eyes off the screen. For weeks we had hoped that military action would begin and that it would convince Iraq to give up its ludicrous claim that Kuwait was its 19th province.

During the 42-plus days that followed the initial air strike, we were never more than a few minutes away from CNN. We frequently tuned in to coverage 18-20 hours a day, one day after another. Sometimes we actually took turns sleeping to be sure we did not miss a single important event, all the time hoping that each day would be the last and that our friends in Kuwait would finally be liberated.

Most of the American wives and families of those Kuwaitis we knew in Kuwait managed to leave the country when Saddam Hussein agreed to release foreign hostages. Fortunately, most of the all-Kuwaiti families we knew were outside Kuwait on their annual August holiday when the invasion took place. With the exception of a nephew of Kuwait's Minister of Higher Education, who was seriously injured in a land-mine accident while celebrating Kuwait's liberation, we are unaware of any significant physical misfortune that befell our friends. However, many of our friends suffered significant property damage or the loss of property to looters. Although none of our friends were among the victims of the human atrocities that enraged the world, one of our best friends Dr. Abbas Alikhan, suffered a great deal of mental anguish after allowing two daughters to return home early from their holiday in Turkey, just two days before the invasion.[81] It was almost a month later before Dr. Abbas learned that his daughters were safe with members of his family, who were in Kuwait at the time of the invasion. Thousands of Kuwaitis suffered through this same type of mental anguish, not knowing the whereabouts or having a way to determine the condition of their loved ones in Kuwait.

While in London on business during the fall of 1991, we happened to meet a participant from a 1987 Kuwait Foundation for the Advancement of Sciences (KFAS) seminar in San Francisco. This former student just happened to enter a Sheraton Park Tower Hotel elevator at the same time we did. Even though it had been four years, he recognized us immediately. He was filled with excitement as he shared a Gulf War-related story that left us all standing with our mouths open. It seems that after the Iraqis had been evicted from Kuwait, a small group of American soldiers returning from the front visited one of the *diwaynias* in Kuwait City, asking if anyone knew the people in a photograph they had found. The photo, along with a number of personal and household items had been left behind in one of the Iraqi bunkers near the Iraq-Kuwait border. The soldiers were attempting to find the rightful owner. When the Kuwaiti men at the *diwaynia* saw the picture, they immediately recognized my Kuwaiti friend, so the soldiers left the photo and the personal belongings with them for safe keeping until they could be reclaimed. When my friend returned to his home, these same Ku-

---

[81] Hundreds of Kuwaiti citizens and Kuwait supporters were killed, tortured or wounded. By the summer of 1992, nearly one thousand Kuwaitis remained missing or held by Iraq as prisoners of war.

waitis told him about the American soldiers and showed him the picture that had enabled them to identify the "loot" the soldiers found. He told us he could not believe his eyes! As he finished telling the story, my Kuwaiti friend smiled broadly before informing us that the picture the American soldiers found abandoned in the Iraqi bunker was of my family and all of the 1987 San Francisco seminar participants. Small world!

Kuwait's horrible nightmare officially ended at midnight (EDT) on Wednesday, February 27, 1991.[82] Once the deed was done, once Iraq had been forced to leave Kuwait, the assessment of the extent of the damage to the Kuwaiti infrastructure could begin. Now, without the threat of Iraqi violence, the Kuwaiti people could also begin to assess the substantial personal loss of property and emotional stability. The government leaders and the Royal Family could return to Kuwait and initiate the rebuilding process, a process that even the most optimistic prognosticators estimated would take years and billions of dollars to complete.

There can be no doubt that the Arabian Gulf experience was a living nightmare for the hundreds of thousands of Kuwaitis affected directly or indirectly by the Iraqi aggression as well as for the families of Coalition troops injured or killed while contributing to the fight against tyranny.

However, one person's nightmare can quickly become a dream come true for someone else. This is certainly the case in regard to the massive and far-reaching destruction that was inflicted upon Kuwait

---

[82] Kuwait celebrates February 26 as Liberation Day, since it was on that day that Kuwait City was declared free from Iraqi occupation. It was February 27th when the United Nation's Coalition claimed its mission to remove Iraq from Kuwait was accomplished.

and its economy. The cost to rebuild has been conservatively estimated at between $20 and $25 billion over the next three to five years (original estimate placed the cost at between $50 and $60 billion). These estimates and the expectations of companies hoping to get their "fair share" of the Kuwait rebuilding pie have been described as a businessman's "dream come true." Americans, having taken the lead in assembling and directing the efforts of the Coalition Forces against Saddam Hussein, expect to be awarded a large number of the contracts to assist in Kuwait's rebuilding efforts. Unfortunately, the anticipated windfall for many businesses has been slow in coming. The slow pace is not unusual when doing business in the Middle East and Kuwait is no exception. I can't remember how many times I have heard the word, "Enshalla"[83] when discussing a business arrangement or a pending contract. The pace is slow in the Middle East, but with patience, the opportunities are significant. In contrast to the complaints by many American businessmen, a United States Department of Commerce report dated January 17, 1992 states: "Despite sometimes slow movement in the reconstruction process, many American firms have done well in Kuwait in the post-war period. Those willing to approach the Kuwaiti market systematically have scored some stunning successes."[84]

A great deal of Kuwaiti government attention

---

[83] *Enshalla* is probably the most frequently heard word in Kuwait. Translated *Enshalla* means, "if God is willing" and it is used at the beginning or end of almost every discussion in Kuwait that deals with the future. This "don't worry, God decides anyway" attitude quickly becomes obvious in personal and business activities in Kuwait.

[84] United States exports and contracts in Kuwait exceeded $2 billion in 1991 (twice as much as 1990) and 1992 could reach $3 billion, Seventy percent of all Emergency Recovery Work contracts, worth over $600 million, were awarded to American companies.

has been aimed at bringing some stability back to the internal political and social environment. A new Cabinet was formed, and huge amounts of energy were targeted at getting the school facilities back in pre-invasion functioning order for the opening of school in late August of 1991. Additionally, restoring basic services, such as electricity and water, required focused attention to provide the essential elements of daily life to those already in Kuwait, as well as those thousands that returned soon after Kuwait's liberation.

In the meantime a war of another kind was waged every day: the war to distinguish and rehabilitate the 751 damaged or burning oil wells, thus enabling the Kuwaiti economy to begin generating revenue once again from its most reliable source. The wells were set ablaze by the departing army as its final act of wanton destruction in Kuwait. As of mid-August, 1991, one year after the invasion, more than 220 of the well fires had been extinguished, and the oil field at Ahmadi claimed that not only were all fires out, but that oil was once again being produced. On November 6, 1991, the last of the 751 burning or damaged oil wells was capped bringing to a conclusion an unprecedented mobilization of historical proportions led by American companies.

The cost associated with rebuilding the oil industry in Kuwait is staggering. Kuwait government officials estimated that it would cost an average of $500,000 per well to put the fires out and another $500 million to put the wells back in operating condition. Add to this the potential estimated cost of $7 billion to repair the damage done to the oil refineries, and the scope of the rebuilding effort begins to take shape.

The physical effort is, indeed, monumental. The emotional rebuilding effort may be larger still. Ku-

waitis who remained in Kuwait throughout the occupation, either members of the loosely organized resistance
movement or those who stayed because they could not
leave, have terrible memories of death and torture that
they must still deal with on a daily basis. Kuwaitis who
were out of the country or who left with their families in
the interest of safety have to live with the memory of
what they found upon their return. What was once a
modern, proud country had been pillaged and looted of
many of its worldly possessions. Stores were burned-
out shells. Museums were piles of ashes, and banks and
businesses stood vacant with vaults and cash registers
open. Once-picturesque homes and palaces had been
converted to fortresses with windows blocked up, leaving only a small hole for firing a weapon.

For some, the nightmare may never be over.
People from countries around the world once immigrated to Kuwait in order to earn a comfortable living.
Now many of these same immigrants are no longer
welcome. Palestinians, who have been accused of coop-
erating with Iraq during the occupation of Kuwait, are
being carefully screened before being allowed to remain in Kuwait. Thousands of Iraqis, who once made
significant contributions in the work force and to the
Kuwaiti economy are no longer welcome in Kuwait.
Likewise immigrants from Jordan are considered a risk
to Kuwaiti security based on the strong support they
demonstrated for Iraq. These people, many of whom
contributed a great deal to the growth and prosperity of
Kuwait during the past quarter century, were not Kuwaiti citizens, but in many of their hearts they were
Kuwaiti. Their life work was in Kuwait. They earned
their fortunes and raised their families in Kuwait.

Now, because of a madman from Iraq and because of the greed and violent acts of some of the

immigrants who decided to throw their support to the Iraqi madman, the loyal contributors to the success story we call Kuwait - - the same people who never supported the Iraqi action taken on August 2, 1990 - - have become men, women, and children without a country. Iraqis who failed to support Saddam in his quest for power and riches would face certain death if they attempted to return home and are scattered throughout the world with friends or relatives. The Palestinians had no homeland to begin with and now find themselves in an even worse circumstance than before. Since they have lost the trust of the Kuwaiti people, thousands of Palestinians have immigrated to Jordan and surrounding Arab countries.

Immigrants are not the only ones to suffer as a result of understandable Kuwaiti suspicion. Kuwait, although its government has stated on many occasions that it will enter the recovery period with far less immigrant labor, will need help to accomplish a full recovery. Skilled laborers and experts in professional disciplines will be needed to lead the recovery process. The road to recovery will be long and filled with rough spots and detours. However, Kuwait's government and its people have demonstrated that they are prepared for whatever lies ahead. They are committed to returning Kuwait to its former glory. Based on what this determined little country has accomplished in less than 30 years since becoming an independent State, who is going to tell them it cannot be done?

For the old Kuwait, the nightmare has ended, and the new Kuwait is still a dream. But in Kuwait even the wildest dreams have a habit of coming true.

12

MEETING THE CHALLENGE OF CHANGE

Nobody Ever Said It Was Perfect

Lee R. Lambert

*"I like the dreams of the future better than
the history of the past."*

Patrick Henry

Kuwait is rapidly approaching the thirtieth anniversary of the formal ratification of its Constitution by His Highness the Amir, Abdallah Al-Salem Al-Sabah on November 11, 1962. The growth and progress that have been achieved in this short time are truly remarkable, especially considering that these achievements have come within the context of a strict Islamic society. Although Kuwait's Constitution clearly states that Kuwait is a democracy, in the eyes of many Americans, Kuwait has a long way to go before it can truly claim that it is a wholly democratic government. In the Arabian Gulf region, however, Kuwait is clearly recognized for its willingness to adapt and modernize its governmental process within the existing cultural constraints.

Kuwait's leaders acknowledge that in the Western sense, their country is in a state of continued democratic growth and evolution. Achieving total democracy, as defined by Americans, presents a formidable challenge for Kuwaitis and their government. Arab tradition and the strong Islamic influence provides a cultural framework that is drastically different from the

United States. Although certainly sensitive to the observations and constructive criticism of those outside the Gulf region, members of the Kuwaiti government are naturally most concerned about the feelings and desires of their own people - - the constituency they are pledged to serve.

During my many visits to Kuwait, I have attempted to take the pulse of the Kuwaiti people regarding the governmental process currently in place. I have engaged in many private conversations, as well as spirited debates at numerous well-attended *diwaniyahs* where the primary topic of discussion centered around the Kuwaiti government and how it might be improved.[85]

With the exception of a few outspoken "everything-is-wrong" radicals, a personality type which I have encountered in every country I have visited as well as at home in America, the thrust of the discussions generally gravitated to a central theme: a desire for expanded representation of the people in the governmental process. Within this central theme, the major criticisms I heard voiced most often concern nepotism, absolute monarchy and severely limited voting privileges.

Technically speaking, Kuwait's Constitution is somewhat ambivalent on the subject of democracy. On

---

[85] It was the post-war U.S. Ambassador, Edward Gnehm, Jr.'s attendance at local *diwaniyahs* and discussion of democracy in the spring of 1992 that prompted a surprising reaction from Kuwait National Council Speaker Abdul-Aziz Al-Masaeed: "America did not bring us back to our country. If it weren't for the wisdom of our government and the help of Saudi Arabia, the Gulf Cooperation Council, Egypt and Syria, we wouldn't have been liberatede". Kuwaitis at all government levels and from all walks of life immediately refuted the Aziz Al-Masaeed "personal" statement and emphasized the deep gratitude and appreciation they feel for the United States and the men and women who helped liberate Kuwait.

the one hand, Article 6 of the Constitution states, "The System of Government in Kuwait shall be democratic, under which sovereignty resides in the people, the source of all powers." On the other hand, Article 4 states, "Kuwait is a hereditary Amirate, the succession to which shall be in the descendents of the late Mubarak Al-Sabah." Most political experts agree that, in reality, Kuwait is a form of constitutional monarchy. Executive power is vested in the Amir. He exercises his power through The Council of Ministers and the Prime Minister, together with the Crown Prince, form the Kuwaiti Cabinet (the equivalent to the President's Cabinet in the United States). The Cabinet is headed by the Prime Minister, who, in Kuwait's history has also been the Crown Prince and designated heir-apparent to the position of Amir. The Prime Minister is appointed by the Amir, and the respective Ministers are appointed by the Prime Minister.

It is the appointment of Ministers by the Crown prince/Prime Minister which engenders the most frequent charges of nepotism. Some Kuwaiti citizens frequently voice displeasure regarding choice of Ministers and, once chosen, the performance of the particular Minister in his area of responsibility. Some Kuwaitis suggest that the Royal Family members or individuals with close ties to the Royal Family are not always the most qualified for these Minister appointments, and thus, they are not convinced those selected will do a good job of representing the best interests of the average Kuwaiti citizen.

One if the critical elements in any democratic society is an effective system of "checks & balances." On paper, Kuwait's Constitution has addressed this critical element through the creation of a National Assembly or Parliament made up in part of representatives determined through the free election process. Candidates for these National Assembly posts must be literate male Kuwaiti citizens at least 21 years of age. This constitutionally mandated National Assembly is composed of 50 elected positions plus all of the appointed Ministers.[86]

The National Assembly, like the Congress of the United States, serves as representatives of people living in defined districts in Kuwait. Also like its American counterpart, the National Assembly prepares and approves legislation before sending it to the Amir for ratification. The Amir has much the same veto power as the President of the United States, and as in the United States, the National Assembly can override an Amiri veto with a two-thirds vote. Unlike the U.S. system, however, the Amir can issue decrees that have the effect of law. In the event that the Amir issues such a decree, the Constitution requires him to place it before the National Assembly at the next regularly scheduled session for approval (the National Assembly meets twice a week during an eight month session). In the meantime, while awaiting National Assembly review and approval, the decree has the effect of law.

The most significant complaint I have heard concerning Kuwait's governmental system surrounds the National Assembly issue. Under the terms of the Kuwaiti Constitution, as clearly stated in Article 107, the Amir has the authority to dissolve the National Assembly when he feels it is prudent and in the best interest of the nation. On two occasions, once in 1976 and again in 1986, an Amir has chosen to take this drastic step. The first time the National Assembly was dissolved, then

---

[86] In 1990 a National Council was established with 50 elected members and 25 Government appointed members. Considered illigitament by many, the National Council will cease operation following the 1992 Kuwait elections.

Amir Sabah Al-Salem Al-Sabah (12th ruler of Kuwait), cited "unjust attacks and denunciation against ministers by the members" as the primary justification. A decade later his successor and current Amir, Jaber Al-Ahmed Al-Jaber Al-Sabah, used some of the same reasoning along with the continued political unrest and uncertainty in the Gulf region to once again dissolve the Kuwaiti law making body. The Amir had warned the members of the National Assembly that the situation was becoming very sensitive and that continued non-productive friction between the Cabinet and the 50 National Assembly members would not be tolerated.

The Kuwaiti Constitution provides a "check" on the Amir's power, as the same constitutional article that gives the Amir the authority to dissolve the Assembly also specifically requires that a new National Assembly shall be elected within a period not to exceed two months from the date of the dissolution. In both the cited cases of the National Assembly dissolution, however, this constitutional requirement was not met. In the first dissolution of 1976, the new National Assembly was not elected until February of 1982, a period of six years. In the second dissolution of 1986, elections had just been conducted when Iraq invaded Kuwait and was subsequently declared void. Once Kuwait was liberated from Iraqi occupation on February 27, 1991, there was pressure to schedule the election of a new National Assembly, but the Amir, concerned that it would take some months for the country to go through the healing process and for things to return to a near-normal state, wisely delayed the elections until approximately October of 1992.

In a related issue, many Kuwaitis are requesting expansion of the voting privileges to include all Kuwaiti citizens, not just those males who can trace their heritage to 1920. This extremely selective method of determining who was eligible to vote in the 1990 election for the National Assembly resulted in less than one-tenth of the total 830,000 Kuwaiti citizens[87] being eligible while none of the 1.3 million immigrants were eligible. The Kuwaiti people are pressing the government to rethink this entire voting issue, and many are strongly urging them to grant women the right to vote as well.[88]

When pressed on the woman's voting issue, the Crown Prince/Prime Minister, Sheikh Saad Al-Abdallah Al-Salem Al-Sabah, says it is clearly a matter to be considered. You can be sure that the women who remained in Kuwait and suffered through the terrible experience of the Iraqi occupation will not let their government ignore their belief that they have earned the right to have a say in a government they helped save. Kuwait's ambassador to the United States, Sheikh Saud Nasser Al-Sabah, supports expansion of voting rights for Kuwaiti women. The ambassador was quoted in the February 28, 1992 issue of *U.S.A. Today*, "The time has come to end the nation's country club government run by upper-class males."

On the broader issue of women's rights, Kuwait proudly points out that it has been the leader in the Gulf region in many categories, including education (more than half of the students at Kuwait University are female), working outside the home, and driving a car.

---

[87] Estimates made in 1990 place the number of Kuwaiti males meeting the existing voter eligibility requirements to be about 65,000, or about eight percent.

[88] Kuwait finds itself in a "Catch-22" situation regarding the granting of voting rights to women. Kuwait leaders have indicated a desire to have women vote, however, allowing women voting rights requires a change in the Constitution of the State of Kuwait. The Constitution can only be changed by the National Assembly, which is to be elected in October, 1992.

Kuwaiti leaders quickly remind their American critics that it took the United States nearly 150 years to grant its women citizens the right to vote! Kuwaitis strongly believe that their country has yet to reach its political and democratic maturity, and they firmly believe that Kuwaiti women are very much a part of that maturing process.

Anyone who mistakenly thinks women are second class citizens in Kuwait obviously has not had the opportunity to see first hand how much they are respected and how well they are treated. Except for some in the rapidly disappearing older generation, the perception that all Kuwaiti women walk dutifully behind their husbands, waiting to carry out his every request, could not be further from the truth. Many Kuwaiti women occupy important decision-making positions in the work force and the government, and the modern Kuwaiti family structure essentially treats husband and wife as equals. Much work remains to be done to achieve true equality and a lasting democracy in Kuwait, but the significant progress that has been made during recent years should not be discounted.

Another issue that concerns voting, but goes beyond simple voting rights is the much broader question of granting Kuwaiti citizenship to resident aliens. Kuwait is a proud nation that guards its citizenship with extreme care. But within the fabric of Kuwaiti society, there are also some proud immigrants who have lived and worked in Kuwait, raised their families in Kuwait, and very well may die in Kuwait. Many of these immigrants have been major contributors to the social and economic prosperity that Kuwait and its citizens have enjoyed since becoming independent in 1961. Some of these immigrants remained in Kuwait during the Iraqi invasion and contributed to the Kuwaiti resistance movement. These same devoted immigrants feel strongly that the Kuwaiti government should grant them the opportunity to be recognized formally and legally as Kuwaiti citizens.

Under the present system it is technically possible to become a "naturalized" Kuwaiti citizen,[89] but the process is very subjective and extremely long, and even after the long wait, chances of an individual being granted Kuwaiti citizenship are slim. In the case of a non-Kuwaiti woman married to a Kuwaiti citizen, for example, the woman is not automatically granted Kuwaiti citizenship. In the wife example, a special committee would conduct an investigation of the wife; and if the information obtained shows no reason she should be denied Kuwaiti citizenship, she would be given all rights and benefits afforded to any other native Kuwaiti - - after a fifteen year waiting period! If the woman's husband should die during the fifteen year waiting period, she would be considered a foreigner by the government. Although she would ordinarily be allowed to remain in Kuwait, collect her rightful share of any inheritance, and retain custody of the children, the possibility of being deported would always exist. If she should be deported or chose to leave Kuwait for some reason, custody of the children would normally be granted to a member of the deceased Kuwaiti husband's family.

These major issues, along with many other related, but less critical matters, have been discussed

---

[89] An alien can become a naturalized citizen of the United States through a formal process that requires: (1) a petition for naturalization, (2) an investigation and interview, and (3) final hearings in court. The alien seeking citizenship must have lived in the U.S. for five years, be of good moral character, and demonstrate attachment for the principles of the U.S. Constitution.

with the Kuwaiti leadership. The Amir, the Crown Prince/Prime Minister, and the Cabinet have repeatedly pledged their commitment to respond to the concerns of the Kuwaiti people. Following the Iraqi invasion and Saddam Hussein's claim that dissatisfied Kuwaiti citizens had invited him to come onto Kuwait, Kuwait convened the Kuwaiti People's Conference in Jeddah, Saudi Arabia, October 13-15, 1990, at which time the government pledged to the people its commitment to increasing democratization in what would become the new Kuwait. His Highness, the Crown Prince, told the huge gathering of citizens and officials, "Kuwait will take the necessary measures to consolidate democracy and allow for more extensive participation . . ."

However, no matter how many complaints I hear about the Royal Family and the Kuwait government, no matter how vocal the complainer is, no matter how strongly the concerns are stated, each time I ask if the Royal Family should be ousted and new leadership put in place, the answer is always the same - - "No!" Followed quickly by something like, "We've never wanted the Amir to step down. He and his fellow leaders have done an excellent job of providing for us and our children. All we really want is the opportunity for more representation and participation in the governmental process." In their opinion this does not seem like too much to ask.

The eyes of the world, especially Americans who sacrificed a great deal to turn back the Iraqi tyrant, will be watching as the "old" Kuwait gradually is transformed into the "new" and improved Kuwait. Interest will be high in observing whatever substantive changes are made. Efforts to reconstitute the Kuwait society to the pre-August 2, 1990 condition will, most likely, be unacceptable to the Kuwaiti people.

The Al-Sabah government will have to face the challenges of dealing with perceived separation of Kuwait's population into two distinct groups: those who stayed in Kuwait during the Iraqi occupation and those who fled the country. Strong feelings among those who remained behind to endure the months of physical and mental anguish must be carefully considered in determining the ultimate shape of the new Kuwait.

Claims of mismanagement, corruption, and neglect by those in the so-called "opposition", must also be addressed. Somehow, the Al-Sabah government must achieve a balance in addressing the opposing objectives of the Islamic Constitutional Movement, a small group of Kuwaitis who advocate a return to *Sharia* or strict Islamic Law, and those in the Democratic Forum, who represent a loose coalition of small opposition groups seeking expanded democracy.

Despite these and other political challenges, Kuwait now has a unique chance to turn this tragic Iraqi invasion and occupation into a once-in-a-lifetime opportunity to begin again. The Kuwaiti people will rely on their leadership to build on the good from the past and to eliminate the bad. A leading young Kuwaiti lawyer said it best, "This is a critical period in our lives, we will never have such a chance again. We must not lose it."

In addition to these crucial political and Constitutional challenges, the new Kuwait must also face some serious practical problems which existed long before the Gulf War and, if not solved, will have a significant negative impact on the quality of life in Kuwait in the years ahead.

Based upon my observation, some of the most

urgent of these problems, which require Kuwait's immediate attention and a substantial investment of both human and financial resources, concern traffic control and safety, housing, and the general composition and motivation of the work force.

When it comes to driving skill and safety, Kuwait has a problem - - a very serious and deadly problem. I have driven on the streets of Paris, London, Sydney, Amsterdam, Brussels, Vienna, Frankfurt, Geneva, Aukland, and most major cities in the United States and Canada. But, I have never driven anywhere that begins to compare to the streets of Kuwait City for pure terror. The most obvious way to verify my claim is to spend a few hours in an automobile working your way through the city streets. The experience leaves me stunned. Driving in Kuwait reminds me of the times I used to spend as a boy taking my turn in the traveling carnival's bumper car ride - - except, in Kuwait, the cars are real, and they are hurtling toward you at speeds of 70-80 miles an hour in town and much faster on the expressways.

A recent study conducted by the Kuwait Foundation for the Advancement of Sciences (KFAS) quantified the severity of the problem that everyone knows to exist. The study revealed that during a ten-year period ending in 1988 there were 223,084 auto accidents in Kuwait, or an average of 26 accidents every hour of every day, every day of the week, every week of the year. The impact on human life as a result of these accidents is appalling. During the ten-year period mentioned above, 21,132 people were injured seriously enough to require medical attention. But even more devastating was the loss of 4,237 lives in that same ten-year period. These numbers seem small when compared to 45,000 killed and 1.7 million injured each year in the United States; but in light of the small Kuwaiti population the severity of the highway carnage becomes clear.[90] The personal injury and death figures equate to five people seriously injured and one Kuwaiti resident killed every two hours during the past 10 years. In fact, dying in an auto accident was the second leading cause of death in Kuwait during this same ten-year period. Of the total 46,797 deaths in Kuwait, almost ten percent were directly attributable to an automobile-related incident. The only single killer that took more lives in Kuwait during this same period was heart disease. Statistically speaking, the chances of being killed on Kuwaiti roads are eleven times greater than dying in a fire and thirty-one times greater than being murdered.

The loss of 4,237 lives is certainly a sad and unnecessary waste of humanity. But in Kuwait's case, the loss is even more tragic because the majority of the deaths and serious , debilitating injuries occur among the ranks of the young, the same segment of the population who holds the key to its future growth and prosperity. As a nation that lays its hopes for the future at the feet of its younger generation, Kuwait has begun to recognize that its autos and roadways are truly the enemy of the youth. As one official put it, "Our streets have become a theater of death and destruction."

The KFAS study attempted to investigate the Kuwait traffic problem by considering three specific areas: driver education, highway engineering, and law enforcement. The study concluded that considerable deficiencies exist in all three areas and that substantial resources must be invested in the years ahead if Kuwait hopes to put an end to the highway problem. From what

---

[90] The United States has a density of about 40 cars for every mile of paved roadway, while Kuwait's density is 200 cars for each mile of roadway.

I have seen in Kuwait, however, and from what I have observed in regard to the Kuwaiti drivers, especially the young men, I think the biggest contributor to the Kuwaiti traffic problem is attitudinal. Because of their considerable wealth, young Kuwaitis have grown up having everything they want when they want it. They are not fond of rules or regulations and often ignore them if they do not allow them the freedom to which they have become accustomed. This same attitude shows up behind the wheel of a car. Generally speaking, my experience suggests that Kuwaiti drivers do not think the traffic rules apply to them. This attitude, combined with the incredible number of cars on the road, significantly increases any driver's odds of becoming involved in an accident.

Serious and timely efforts at improving driver education, road engineering, and law enforcement will certainly help to resolve Kuwait's traffic problems; but until a major shift in the Kuwaiti driver's attitude toward following the rules and regulations can be realized, the problem - - and serious injuries and deaths that result - - will not be eliminated.

Another major problem facing the new Kuwait concerns a potentially serious housing shortage. As has been cited in Chapter 6, Kuwait has a stated goal of providing housing for all its citizens. Considerable progress has been made toward achieving this enviable goal. In fact, the population density for Kuwaitis has been reduced from 3.5 people per room in 1961 to approximately one person per room in 1989. Using this statistic as an indicator, I found that Kuwait now ranks among the most highly developed countries in the world.

However, a review of the demographics of the Kuwaiti population reveals that a significant, potential housing problem is hiding beneath the surface. According to Kuwait's 1986 Annual Statistical Abstract, sixty percent of Kuwait's total population are between the ages of four and twenty years. Ten percent are between fifteen and twenty years old. Based on these figures, the government projects that within the next four to five years as many as 40,000 young men will marry and add their names to the already-lengthy list of those waiting for government housing.

The housing shortage problem has not been overlooked by the government - quite to the contrary. Housing has been a top priority for several years. The latest Kuwaiti Five Year Plan, ending in 1990, called for the completion of almost 17,000 new houses for Kuwaiti citizens. Plans for an additional 12,000 were in place at the time of the Iraqi invasion. But even with these high priority production rates, the number of new families expected to go on the waiting list, added to those who have already been waiting for up to seven years for their house to be completed, indicates that a serious housing shortage will exist within the coming decade.

A great deal of attention must be given to overcoming this housing problem in the coming years. This may be one of the government's biggest challenges, especially in light of the tremendous financial and labor resources required to simply return Kuwait to its pre-invasion condition.

In addition to the obvious financial constraint, the fact that the number of immigrant workers in Kuwait has been drastically reduced following the Gulf War may further slow the already ridiculously long residential construction time. Earlier attempts by the Ministry of Housing to reduce house size, incorporate prefab construction techniques, and introduce multi-unit, single family housing complexes all proved unacceptable to the fussy prospective Kuwaiti homeowner. Perhaps, under these new circumstances, the Kuwaiti consumers will reconsider implementing these and other cost and time saving approaches in building a house.

Perhaps the most critical question yet to be answered about the new Kuwait is, "Who will do the work?" In the pre-invasion Kuwait, it was the hundreds of thousands of immigrants who assumed this role. These immigrant workers served tea and fresh juice to people in the work place, *souks*, and government offices. The immigrants drove Kuwaiti women and children and foreign visitors to social and business functions. The immigrants repaired cars and pumped gas. The immigrants taught school and filled thousands of entry level and middle management jobs in government and private industry. The immigrants also cooked food, served food, and then cleaned up the mess. I have had the opportunity to become friendly with some of these immigrant drivers, managers and domestic workers; and none of them ever indicated they were mistreated or abused in any way. In fact, everyone I spoke to was proud of the contribution he or she was making to the Kuwait quality of life.

Things have changed in Kuwait! Early projections suggest fewer than half the 1.3 million immigrant workers from 139 different countries will be among the estimated 1.5 million post-war, new Kuwait population. If this projection is accurate, then I must ask again, "Who will do the work?" In this regard Kuwait's government is facing three problems: of those immigrants who remained in Kuwait, whom should be allowed to stay; of those who fled the country in the early weeks of the occupation, whom should be allowed to return; and, perhaps most difficult, how will those who left and are now welcome back in Kuwait, be convinced it is wise to return?[91] These questions must be answered before it can be determined who will do the work.

In the pre-invasion days, no-self respecting Kuwaiti would stoop so low as to engage in physical labor to earn his living. Kuwaitis have been educated and trained to investigate, manage, direct, or teach. Immigrants did the work. Even Kuwait's Ambassador to the United States, Sheikh Saud Nasser Al-Sabah, admits, "Most Kuwaitis are spoiled beyond imagination." Former Minister of Planning, Suleiman Mutawa concurred, stating, "We were the pampered product of an affluent society taken to the nth degree."

Tareq Al-Suwaidan, leader of one of the small so-called opposition groups in Kuwait, told *Time* magazine in a 1990 interview, "Ours was a culture of dependency." Al-Suwaidan went on to say, "The only way to exit the trap of dependency is to make it impossible for people to be reliant on others. Most of those who have done the real work in the past will have to go, Then", he concludes, "there will be no choice. The rest of us will have to do the hard work."

We have talked with some of our friends in Kuwait, and they verify that a shift in attitude concerning work is, in fact, taking place, at least as far as household duties are concerned. Two married couples we know (American wives and Kuwaiti husbands) have not replaced their household workers and are managing to survive nicely as they have assumed the duties of house cleaning, watching the kids, cleaning the pool, and washing the clothes.

The challenge facing the Kuwaiti government is

---

[91] As of May, 1992 Kuwait government officials have indicated more than 600,000 foreign workers have returned to jobs in Kuwait.

this: how do you motivate a society that has grown up under these unrealistic conditions? How do you change a state of mind that accepts as fact that Kuwaitis do not work? Ambassador Saud posed a similar question, "how do you get people to actually stop being lazy?" For Kuwaitis, the old days are gone forever. A new day has dawned.

The need for change facing Kuwait is massive. It amounts to a major cultural overhaul of a magnitude perhaps never undertaken by any country in modern times. In this sort of cultural shift, it soon becomes obvious that all things are linked. When one thing changes, everything else changes accordingly. Planning for this type of a behavioral modification at a nationwide level must be thorough and precise, with all potential impact areas meticulously evaluated.

Once the idea has been accepted that Kuwaitis should begin to shoulder their fair share of work, the key to long-term success will be in how effectively the Kuwaiti educational system is able to modify its approach and offer programs that will prepare Kuwaitis to assume their critical new roles in the work force. Currently, those responsible for the various educational sectors in Kuwait are actively investigating methods, such as monetary incentives, guaranteed jobs, and faster advancement, to name a few, to insure that Kuwaitis respond favorably and that Kuwait's objectives in this area will be met.

Another central issue dealing with Kuwaiti rights and freedoms is in the area of the press and the restrictions and constraints thereon. The Kuwaiti government proudly quotes Article 37 of its Constitution: "Freedom of the Press, printing and publishing shall be guaranteed in accordance with the conditions and manner specified by law," However, the Constitution also makes it clear in Article 2 that, "The religion of the State is Islam, and the Islamic *Sharia* shall be a main source of legislation." The difficulty in assessing the freedom of the Kuwait press comes in interpreting what is acceptable according to the Islamic *Sharia* and the general principles of Islam. Frequently, Kuwaiti newspapers will not print, or be allowed to print, what is considered to be objectionable material. Often information they print has portions "blacked out" by Kuwaiti censors. News stories that are critical of the government, or actions taken by the government, are often victims of the censor's pen, but generally, Kuwaiti censorship is exercised on imported books, magazines, and newspapers.

I remember well looking through issues of *Life* and *Time* magazines purchased in Kuwait and noticing advertisements featuring scantily clad women. However, each time black marking pens had been used to "cover" any portion of a woman's skin that was exposed. My family and I still joke about what a boring job it must be to find all the pictures of women with skin showing and to make sure they are "properly clad" in solid black. The chance of finding any published material in Kuwait that even remotely resembles what Americans define as pornographic is nil.

When the Lamberts began traveling to Kuwait, this strict approach to censorship was also extended to all television programming. Profanity and any scene that remotely suggested anything sexual - - even a simple kiss - - was edited out or "bleeped" from the broadcast. In our last few trips, however, we noticed a more liberal attitude toward censorship on the television. In some programs (Kuwaiti television viewers now receive a wide variety of programming, including second-run movies in English and dubbed Arabic and syndicated shows from the United States such as "The Cosby Show and Teenage Mutant Ninja Turtles") members of the cast were barely clothed, and in some cases profanity occurred. When we asked our friends if Kuwait had actually relaxed its tough censorship position in relation to moral issues, we were told, "Definitely not, but some of the television programs that are shown are available via satellite and are not always subjected to the same tight screening applied to local programming."

Critics of the current Kuwaiti government and its policies frequently raise this censorship issue as proof that Kuwait does not, in fact, have a free-press society. Some claim it is impossible to have what we in the Western world consider a free press under the cultural constraints inherent in a State whose legislation is based on the Islamic *Sharia*.

Kuwait will, I am sure, continue to selectively censor its press in accordance with these religiously driven criteria. However, Kuwait's Minister of Information, as well as members of the local press, is quick to point out that for many years Kuwait has had the most liberal and comprehensive press and information services in the Arab world. For example, at the time of the Iraqi invasion, Kuwait readers could choose from 111 different newspapers and magazines published in a dozen different languages. This number included eight newspapers published daily in Kuwait. These publications currently provide Kuwaiti residents with coverage on all aspects of life in cultures throughout the world. The extensive amount of information readily available in Kuwait is an achievement of which Kuwaiti officials are very proud. Everyone involved from the Ministry of Information pledges to continue this improvement whenever possible.

Nobody in Kuwait has ever told me their country is perfect. Every country and every government has room for improvement. Kuwait is no different! The Kuwaiti people understand, and the Kuwaiti government understands. Together they are working to make the new Kuwait the best it can be.

CONCLUSION

Our personal impressions of "The Other Kuwait" are based on our experiences in the old Kuwait. The old Kuwait was an exciting place to visit. Visiting the old Kuwait was an educational adventure beyond compare. The old Kuwait was a unique blend of modern conveniences and ancient Arab/Islamic tradition. The old Kuwait was constantly looking for ways to improve. The old Kuwait was a fun place to make new friends and share personal and cultural anecdotes.

What does the future hold for the new Kuwait?

This is the question on everyone's mind in Kuwait and throughout the world as this tiny Arab Emirate seeks to recover from the physical and emotional damage inflicted by the Iraqi invasion. Will the recovery simply mean a return to the status quo, or will the Kuwaiti leadership use this opportunity to take Kuwait and its people to new heights of accomplishment and worldwide recognition?

Our eyes, and the eyes of the world will be watching with great anticipation to behold the new Kuwait.

ACKNOWLEDGMENTS

There so many people to whom we owe thanks for making this book a reality, but none stands higher on the list than our good friend, and incredibly talented and patient editor, Connie Berry. Her editorial skill, coupled with a sincere desire to learn about Kuwait and its people, provided the unbiased and constantly probing review that contributed immeasurably toward bringing this book to life. At one point, following a particularly long and difficult editing session, Connie confessed to us, "I feel like I have just wrestled a Kuwaiti to the ground and forced him to volunteer the last bit of detailed information I needed." No amount of thanks can repay her for the countless hours she has devoted to the project.

Foremost among the Kuwaitis who must be cited for their individual contributions are Dr. Ali A. Al-Shamlan, Kuwait's Minister of Higher Education, and Adnan and Charlotte Al-Abdulmuhsen, three of the best friends anyone could ever hope for.

From January 8, 1991, when we originally advised Kuwait of our intentions to write this book, Dr. Ali A. Al-Shamlan has been our champion, encouraging us to be patient, but persistent, while he represented our important project to the appropriate Kuwaiti Ministry of Information officials, without whose support and cooperation this book could not have been completed. Dr. Ali's unyielding enthusiasm, support and encouragement for this project gave us the strength to carry on during frequent times of delay and frustration.

We owe a special debt of gratitude to Adnan Al-Abdulmuhsen who, in addition to applying his impressive artistic talent in designing the book's cover, was our fountain of Kuwaiti and Islamic knowledge. Whenever we were not sure of the accuracy of our information, whenever we needed more detail, or whenever

Connie challenged us with questions neither of us had considered, we would simply phone or fax Adnan in Kuwait City. In a matter of a few days he would provide the answers. In total, we posed more than 200 difficult queries to Adnan, for which he provided 200 thoroughly researched, refined, and accurate answers. Without Adnan's and Charlotte's undaunted, moral support, and investigative efforts, the educational value of this book would have been significantly reduced.

We also want to thank our good friends, Dr. Abbas Alikhan, Director of Symposia and Cultural Affairs at the Kuwait Foundation for the Advancement of Sciences (KFAS), and Dr. Ali Al-Tarrah, in the Cultural Division of the State of Kuwait's Embassy in Washington, D.C. for their constant encouragement and moral support, as well as their role as middle-men for our frequent communications with our sources in Kuwait.

Finally, we must thank the rest of the Lambert family, Carolyn, Davin, and Marnie, for the patience and support they exhibited as we ever-so-slowly accomplished our writing assignments. From Marnie's perfect title choice, which came after months of our failure to identify an appropriate title, to helpful suggestions, to pointed criticisms, to simply sharing their memories of fun times in Kuwait, all of them have, in their own special ways, made an invaluable contribution to the finished product.

Although we drew on many references during the nearly one year it took us to research and write this book, the primary source of our information came from our own experiences and observations during our many trips to Kuwait. Once we started writing, we were, and continue to be, very thankful for the enthusiasm and constant encouragement of our many friends throughout the United States, Great Britain, and Kuwait, who convinced us that we must finish our story about The Other Kuwait - - the Kuwait that the Lambert family has come to know and love.

BIBLIOGRAPHY

Abu-Hakima, Ahmad Mustafa, *The Modern History of Kuwait 1750-1965*, Luzac & Company, Ltd., london, 1983.

Al-Akkas, Muhammad A., Editor, *Welcome to Arabia*, 2nd ed. Al-Ebtehar Press, Dammam, Saudi Arabia, 1990.

Al-Jumah, Haider Hassan, T*he Kuwaiti Stock Market Crisis*, Kuwait Press. Kuwait, 1986.

Business Week Magazine, "Operation Desert Market: A Thirst for U.S. Goods," *Business Week*, February 17, 1992.

Christi, Shaykh, "Salat; The Muslim Postures of Prayer, (Islam: Beyond Stereotypes - Special Section)", *Whole Earth Review*, Winter, 1985.

Cupp, David T. and John Frazer, "Kuwait: Aladdin's Lamp of the Middle East." *National Geographic*, May 1969.

Darwish, Adel, and Alexendar Gregory, *Unholy Babylon The Secret History of Saddam's War*, Victor Gollancz ltd., London, 1991.

Economist Magazine, "In the Shia Shadow, (Opposition to Shia Muslims Takes Root in Kuwait)," *The Economist*, April, 18, 1987.

Elmer-Dewitt, Philip, "A Man Made Hell on Earth." *Time*, March 18, 1991.

Farah, Abdulrahim, Editor, *Kuwait*, United Nations Department of Public Information, New York, New York, 1991.

Friedman, Norman, *Desert Victory The War for Kuwait*, United States Naval Institute, Annapolis, Maryland, 1991.

Forbes Magazine, "The Party of Ali, (Shiite Muslims)," *Forbes*, April 12, 1982.

Gnehm, Edward, "Americans and Kuwaitis: Business Partners for Life," *Business America*, March 9, 1992.

Hawkins, Dana; Louise Lief, Eva Pomice, Leslie Mandel-Viny, "Kuwait's Other Cloud," *U.S. News & World Report*, April, 1991.

Helminski, Edmund, "Islam: Blind Spot of the West, (Islam: Beyond Stereotypes - Special Section)", *Whole Earth Review*, 1985.

Horwitz, Tony, *Baghdad Without A Mao and Other Misadventures in Arabia*, Penguin Group, New York, New York, 1991.

Jarallah, Ahmed, Editor, *Expats Guide to Kuwait*, 3rd ed. Almuna Publishers, Safat, Kuwait, 1987.

Jolidon, Laurence, "USA's Bill for Gulf War: $7.3 Billion," *USA Today*, May 6, 1992.

Kelly, J.B., *Arabia The Gulf & The West*, George Weidenfield and Nicolson Limited, 1980.

Kramer, Michael, "Kuwait Chaos and Revenge", *Time*, March 18, 1991

Kramer, Michael, "Toward A New Kuwait," *Time*, December 24, 1990.

Kuwait, Ministry of Information, Editor, *Kuwait Facts and Figures, 1988*. Ministry of Information Publishing, Safat, Kuwait, 1988.

Kuwait, Ministry of Information, Editor, *The Story of Currency in Kuwait*, Ministry of Information Publishing, Safat, Kuwait, 1984.

Kuwait, Ministry of Information and Al-Arabi Magazine, Editors, *Kuwait on the March*, Ministry of Information Publishing, Safat, Kuwait, 1989.

Kuwait, Ministry of Planning, Editor, *Statistical Review 1988*, Ministry of Planning Publishing, Safat, Kuwait, 1989.

Lamb, David, *The Arabs Journeys Beyond the Mirage*, Random House, New York, New York, 1988.

Mansfield, Peter, *Kuwait Vanguard of the Gulf*, Hutchinson Publishing Co. Ltd., London, 1990.

Sapsted, David, *Modern Kuwait*, Macillan London Limited, London, 1980

Scarce, Jennifer M., *The Evolving Culture of Kuwait*, Royal Scottish Museum, Edinburgh, Scotland, 1985.

United States, United States Information Agency, *Seven Months to Freedom*, USIA, Washington, D.C., 1991

U.S. News and World Report Magazine, "Shiites: At the Cutting Edge of Islamic Revolution," *U.S. News & World Report*, July 1, 1985.

INDEX